Vina

Suzanne Cara

Ti ringrazio molto, il tuo interesse per mia mamma, un tesoro come tutte le mamme del mondo.

Baci e Abbraccio

Columbia MO 18 marzo, 2024

Published by Compass Flower Press
an imprint of AKA-Publishing
Columbia, Missouri

ISBN 978-1-942168-57-7 Trade Paperback

Vina

A Brooklyn Memoir

Joseph C. Polacco

To Nancy, a woman with energy radiating from within, much as Vina's light.

Contents

Introduction

> About once a month I run across a person who radiates an inner light. These people can be in any walk of life. They seem deeply good. They listen well. They make you feel funny and valued. You often catch them looking after other people, and as they do so, their laugh is musical and their manner is infused with gratitude. They are not thinking about what wonderful work they are doing. They are not thinking about themselves at all.
> —David Brooks, *The Road to Character*, 2015

When my wife, Nancy Malugani, read David Brooks' words she told me that they described my mother, a woman of Inner Light. Imagine, a cherished Mother-in-Law. My mother, Mom, Vina, left us three years ago after a valiant struggle against recurrent breast cancer. So, why have I undertaken a book about *my* mother? Are not all mothers special? Indeed they are, and my hope is not to advertise my own, so much as to share her light. I do not mourn Vina's passing as premature (she was eighty-seven), nor as particularly painful for her, though it was. I mourn her passing as the dimming of a light in so many people's lives. She was good, she was funny, she could cook, she could sew, knit, and crochet—boy could she sew, knit, and crochet. She, a child of Neapolitan immigrants, could tell Garment District jokes in a Myron Cohen Yiddish accent.

But mostly, Vina was a human beacon. She cared for the various street denizens of Bensonhurst, Brooklyn. She helped Superstorm Sandy victims, comforted battered women and gave Christmas presents to their children. For twenty-two years, to age eighty-six, Vina volunteered at The Holy Family Home, a shelter for the elderly and disabled. She was probably older than many she looked after; she was giving and nurturing even while suffering the effects of recurrent cancer.

I feel that her star is receding, and her light is slowly fading. She meant so much to so many—she was everyone's Aunt Vina—and they reinforce my slanted viewpoint. Aunt Vina was not in the league of Brooks' Dorothy Day, George Marshall, A. Philip Randolph, George Eliot, St. Augustine of Hippo or Samuel Johnson. She did not play on the world stage; hers was family and neighborhood—really the same concept for her. Here I try to capture a few rays of this woman's light: mother, aunt, friend, confidante, grand-mother, Godmother. The last descriptor may sound like a "woman of respect," but Mom was all about selflessness, and not about seeking respect. In fact, our three-room home in back of our linoleum store was known informally as the "The Brooklyn Rescue Mission." Aunt Vina presided.

So, here, just one vignette—no, not Italian for "short Vina story." I was with Mom at Manhattan's South Seaport circa 2007. We had arrived very early to meet cousins Jim and Rosalie Mangano and then to spend a lovely fall day in lower Manhattan. Having time to spare we had a nice long visit, just we two. Time to use the rest room: I awaited Mom outside a long wide corridor leading from the ladies' room. After some time, I could see her leaving, accompanied by a woman of color—a woman I did not know. They were chatting like old friends, and before they got to me the lady and Mom embraced and bade farewell. Naturally, I asked. Seems the lady took her young son into the ladies' room—after all, who would leave a little boy alone in the big city? The lad was naturally upset and uncomfortable. Mom jumped to his rescue, chatted with the boy, mentioned her own two boys, etcetera, etcetera. His mom

Joseph C. Polacco

instinctively trusted my mom and, after tending to her business, she chatted some more with Mom, a conversation that continued until I saw them leaving. So, now you know the rest of the story. But this story is one of many.

This was Mom—Vina—she could capture people's hearts and trust in seemingly ordinary, casual interactions. So, I have written *Vina, A Brooklyn Memoir*—and included many stories contributed by those she touched. The stories also describe the colorful characters Mom associated with in our Brooklyn neighborhood of Bensonhurst. Not all characters are "old broads," as she often called herself and some of her friends, but include men and some very "with it" young people. I realized as I delved, that no matter their age, the women with whom Mom associated were strong and self-sacrificing, much like she was, and I am happy to shed some light on them as well. That such a noble jury comes out so strongly for Mom validates my effort in compiling *Vina*. Mom lived in Brooklyn all her life, but the old country, Southern Italy, the *Mezzogiorno*, was inside her. It shone through all of her interactions, and it figures in the stories of *Vina*.

As I wrote them, I realized that the stories were as much about me as about Mom. During Mom's last fourteen months, I made at least monthly trips back to the old neighborhood. I reconnected with it, and with my Brooklyn inner self. So, I figure in this more than I wanted to at first. But I comfort myself by saying that this is fitting, because Vina's goal, even trumping her charitable efforts, was to raise her two boys well, a challenge in a neighborhood with negative distractions. My brother and I were the motivation for Vina's struggles, travails, and sacrifices—her *raison d'être*. Of course, Mom would never use the French term, not even *ragion d'essere* in "high Italian," or Toscano. She could speak it, when necessary, but was more at home with the dialects of Bari, Naples, and Belmonte Mezzagno, Sicily.

Enjoy Vina's light, her bringing joy and comfort and humor and food and recipes and clothing and, yes, gossip, to the many who loved her. So, this is for the roads that she lit for all of us, and she loved all of us. The narrative is not chronological, the roads not sequential. I have chosen different stretches—those with which I am most familiar, and those stretches on which Mom has left a "verifiable" mark. Many of her fellow travelers are no longer with us, and I wanted to record those still traveling, albeit now without Mom. Most of the above was written before I finished the majority of the stories, and today, about a year on, and on Frank Sinatra's one-hundredth birthday, the old boozy tune goes through my head: "Make it one for my baby, and one more for the road." The stories begat stories, and laid bare layers of dormant memories of incidents, places, and people. I re-traveled many roads, some dark. But here I present a sampler of the much more abundant roads sunlit by Mom.

> "It's quarter to three
> There's no one in the place, except you and me
> So set 'em up Joe, I've got a little story you oughta know
> We're drinking my friend to the end of a brief episode
> Make it one for my baby, and one more for the road."
> Thanks to Johnny Mercer and "The Boss."

Joseph C. Polacco

Vina and Nancy.
Circa 2006.

1. You Don't Have to be Jewish

...to live in Brooklyn. It just rubs off on you. Bensonhurst in the old days was a Jewish-Italian enclave. I was born in 1944 in the Bensonhurst Maternity Hospital on 79th Street and Bay Parkway. The property now houses a Jewish school, and has been across the street from the Jewish Community House—the famous "J"— since 1927. The J was "all-inclusive;" my Sicilian stepdad was a member, along with his buddy Julius Kaplan. Intermarriage between Italians and Jews, not always mutually exclusive labels, was common. Joint mob ventures were not unknown. As a youngster, I thought that as you got older you became Italian, 'cause all the old folks spoke something unintelligible, which I later learned was either Yiddish or some dialect from the Mezzogiorno. But, I *could* recognize blasphemy and foods in either language.

During Mom's last fourteen months I got to know Maimonides Hospital, named for a Sephardic Jewish philosopher of twelfth century Andalucía, Spain. A residue of that Jewish history is a lovely statue of Maimonides in the "Judería" section of Córdoba. The ruling Islamic Moors were kinder to Jewish subjects than were the Catholic rulers, Ferdinand and Isabel, who unified Spain in 1492 and expelled the unconverted Moors. Later came the Inquisition and the expulsion of the Jews. But, back to the present, Maimonides Hospital identifies a medical complex in the very Hasidic Borough Park section of Brooklyn. *You vant to see a melting pot, dah-link?* Just try Maimonides; it's a *minestrone, olla podrida, knaidl* of cultures and religions. It's yarmulkes, do-rags, and bop hats. It's Shabbat from Friday sundown to Sunday mass. *Oy gefilte, Maronna mia.*

Mom's chemo sessions were at the Maimonides Cancer Center.

Later in 2012, when the weather got colder, and Mom weaker, we would opt for a lift home to Bensonhurst from the chemo sessions. One miserable day, rain turning to sleet and ice, and the car service driver was waiting for us, but in a car with a different company name. The car was different, but the driver was typically disheveled, unshaven and, by the time we get in, he's kvetching to the dispatcher. Bad start. But Mom, though just finishing a chemo infusion, is her typical empathetic self, and she doth soothe this savage beast, engaging him in conversation. They are now on the same side, and both agree that the world no longer has morals, and this is the reason we suffer from global warming, wars, AIDS, etcetera, etcetera. The driver identifies himself as Jewish, and says that he grew up in Atlanta, of all places. My mind is racing—an Atlanta Jew, here in Brooklyn? What's the connection? Did Sherman's March through Atlanta, on the way to the sea, beget the Sherman boys? Allie and Allan Sherman were two prominent Jews in my Brooklyn youth—Allie a 1960s New York Giants head coach and Allan, a singer-songwriter ("Hello Muddah Hello Faddah," 1963). Noooooo, couldn't be; but remember that they only needed to be Jewish on their mothers' side.

The driver rouses me from my reverie, turning the conversation to famous Jews and their contributions to American society and to human progress in general. He confirms what I already knew, that the Marx Brothers and Three Stooges were Jewish. I told him, "I'd be proud of the former, and quiet about the latter." Then the litany goes to Alexander Hamilton on the ten-dollar bill I handed him. Hamilton's mother was Jewish; ipso facto, he's Jewish. Our chauffeur learns we're Italian, and he could have *really* scored with the impressive list of famous Jewish-Italian scientists; but no, capo John Gotti's son, and heir apparent, is also Jewish 'cause his dad married a Russian Jewess (Jewessky?). I tell him, 'cause now my dander is up: "Well, he's also Italian, but if you want all of him, we'll trade him to you for cash and two first-round draft choices."

Then, he hits me with his haymaker: "Who was the first Jewish mayor of New York?" I *know* he was expecting me to say our beloved Ed Koch, but I come back with Fiorello (Little Flower) LaGuardia, whose mom was Jewish. I felt like I was back in junior high. But I also felt guilty. I looked over at Mom. I *think* she enjoyed the floorshow. Her inscrutable expression could have signaled that she was still dwelling on the moral depravity of modern society.

Mom spent many years in the New York garment industry. This was material for Myron Cohen, Sam Levinson, and many other beautiful stand-ups. Perhaps not appreciated is that the New York garment industry employed many Jewish *and* Italian seamstresses. For example, collectively they were the majority of victims of the tragic 1911 Triangle Shirtwaist Factory fire. Mom loved the interactions with her Jewish cohorts, some of whom picked up Italian dialect. In turn, Mom's Yiddish-inflected rendition of Myron Cohen sketches was a killer: Could Yiddish "brogue" be emanating from a child of the Mezzogiorno?

One of the great advantages for Italian and Jewish kids in Bensonhurst was access to each other's food. Let me note that the increased density of Chinese in Bensonhurst may have enriched Jewish cuisine. Arthur Olshan, my best buddy in graduate school, was from Far Rockaway—just a little "jag" across the mouth of Jamaica Bay from Coney Island, in Brooklyn territorial waters. Arthur liked to call Chinese takeout "Jewish soul food." His wife Laura definitely agreed, and I think it was Joan Rivers who said that a Jewish mother's call to dinner is "Get in the car." I love people who enjoy a good laugh at their own expense. Of course, Jewish cooking, like Italian, often born of hard times, is much deeper and more complex than a phone call, or a trip to the "House of Ming." Mom made matzoh ball soup, used kasha, and loved the Jewish delis, especially those with daily specials. I know she more than once served me *hamentaschen*, claiming they were *cuccidati*. Both of these delights are dried fruit-filled baked pastries—the former commemorating Purim, Festival of Lots, and the latter, well, we always found them at the Christmas table. I know of Italian pastry chefs forming cuccidati into "three-cornered hats" to capture Jewish clientele.

Over the years, our Bensonhurst neighborhood was becoming more orthodox, and Mom longed for the good ole days when "reformed" Jewry was the norm. We certainly shared with them a ribald sense of humor. Mrs. Epstein ran a clothing (almost schlock, or junk) store, three doors down from our floor-covering business, which was also our 86th Street family home. In 1965 I showed up at that home with a girlfriend from college. We walked the three businesses over to say hello to Mrs. Epstein who was stationed, as usual, in front of a typically spare, understated wood-framed storefront. The vintage "show window" seemed to function more as a visual shield to the goings-on inside. Our stretch of 86th Street was under the shadow of the West End El (elevated), and just like a native, the gal learned to suspend conversation in mid-sentence when the train rumbled overhead. Mrs. Epstein was charmed.

A few days later, Mrs. Epstein called me over and asked if the young lady was Italian. She could have starred in a Broadway remake of *The Ride of the Valkyries*. Upon receiving the expected "No," Mrs. Epstein countered with a conspiratorial look: "Doesn't matter, all women look alike when you turn them upside down (cackle, cackle)." Being in on humor like this let me know I had become a *mensch*—a man. Like Mom, Mrs. Epstein raised two boys, and liked to tell Mom, "Look at the beauty we made in the back of the store."

Jewish humor really is truly amazing considering that incident occurred about twenty years out from the Holocaust and we are now about twenty-five years from Desert Storm. I was born near the end of WWII, and there was a large residue of holocaust survivors in the hood of my adolescence. One of the businesses between our store and Mrs. Epstein's was a laundromat run by a lady with a serial number tattooed on her forearm. She was part of the inventory of the concentration/death camps. To me, she had a perpetual "deer in the headlights" look. She told Mom she would never know how she survived.

Florie Ehrlich was one of Mom's dearest friends. She lived in New York all her life but lost many of her European relatives to the Holocaust; others settled in Israel. Florie was a brave woman who, like Mom, was dealing with a recurrent cancer. Mom knew of her struggles, which Florie kept from many. Florie passed a couple of months before Mom, and her loss was a big blow to Mom's spirits.

Florie was not religious, but lived with her niece Phyllis Diamond, who *was* religious—in a big way. Weeks after Florie's passing, Phyllis and mutual friend Georgette Seminara Adams made one of their visits to Mom's hospital room, and Phyllis said cheerfully, "I was speaking with Florie, and she recommended this nightgown, and the slippers." They were indeed beautiful, and Mom loved them. There was nothing morose about it—we all knew Mom's wish to be buried in a nightgown and slippers, because, as she said, "I am going to sleep." Phyllis, Georgette, and Toni Caggiano sprang for the sleepwear.

Florie and Mom were so close, yet in many ways so different. Florie never married; she had a career in Manhattan and was well-traveled, well-read, and college-educated. She did not get into cooking or eating, and was comfortable with a scotch and a cigarette, smoking right up to her last days. Mom? Well, Mom did read a lot, but her formal education was limited. She did not travel so much, especially considering that my stepdad did not travel very far outside of the neighborhood. Mom, a non-smoker, loved to cook, and she ate well, meaning healthy. She drank wine once in a while, and really never got beyond being a seamstress, career-wise. Marital responsibilities held Mom back from transitioning from Vina the seamstress to *Designs by Vina*, and I will later tell what I have been able to learn about this career path closed.

Florie called Mom every morning at seven. I know, because I was there a lot of those mornings. Florie was my "canary" at a distance. If Mom did not answer, I would have heard immediately, in Columbia, Missouri. They had the most charming conversations, sometimes arguments, but always at a high level, always respectful.

Mom would put me on the phone, and I was usually embarrassed to be hoarse and incoherent at such an ungodly hour. Florie was always happy to chat with me. We would make promises to see each other on my next visit, but alas, in that last year, we ran out of "nexts."

A few years before, when well-read Florie learned I was going to live in the Southern Cone, she mentioned her business trip to Buenos Aires, and gave me a well-documented historical novel, *Woman on Horseback* by William Edmund Barrett (1938). It was about the late 1860s war between Paraguay on one side, and Uruguay, Argentina, and Brazil on the other. This so prepared me for my stay in South America; folks were impressed that an American would know these things. That history helped me understand attitudes and psyches down there.

Florie sometimes accompanied Mom and her cohorts at the weekly Bible studies at Jeanie Gallo's house, and later at the Seminara sisters' place, three houses down. Understand that all these redoubtable ladies were Italian, ergo Roman, Catholics. Rose and Mary Seminara, Georgette Adams, Toni Caggiano, and Jeanie Gallo were a large part of Mom's life—and I will give them their due. And among these ladies was Florie, not even an adopted child; she belonged. Florie read the *New York Times* daily, from cover to cover, and the Bible study was a great opportunity get into "All the news that's fit to print." Once in a while, during heated discussion, she would look up from her paper and make some pithy comment. The Pope wearing a yarmulke was good material. She was hilarious, and so was Mom. They were made for each other.

Bible study more often than not strayed to commentary on politics, current events, public morality—a higher form of gossip. An insight into Florie's religiosity and musical tastes: "When I die I want to go to hell." Okay, I'll bite…. "Because Frank Sinatra is there."

Photo courtesy Georgette Adams

Florie and Vina.
Circa 2006.

2. Julie is 'De Man'

Seems like Julie was always in my life. Julie (Giuli/Giulio) de Ramo is a rough-hewn bear of a man with a large heart. He's in his mid-nineties, and has been a widower for almost twenty years. His Tootsie was loud, brash, very intelligent, and extremely supportive of her husband. She was Vina's good and faithful friend, and she defended her to the extent that she would puncture the façade and posturing of my stepfather—only when he needed it, as all men do, at times. Understandably, Stepdad disliked her—intensely. Julie has been holding the fort without Tootsie, and for all but the last three years, Vina stepped into the breach, buttressing Julie's *forza* (strength). I recall Julie's dutiful 8:00 a.m. phone calls to Mom, on the heels of Florie's. Hence, his chapter follows Florie's. Mom's sweet "Good morning" to Florie morphed into "Julie, don't be ridiculous! You don't remember what you told me yesterday?" The transition was from love to tough love.

Mom and Julie were an energetic comedy team—they argued about *everything*, especially food and food preparation. I was an avid listener to the mostly entertaining "play-by-play." Even when they were on the phone, his voice at the other end was audible in most of Mom's apartment. In the midst of recordings I made of my conversations with Mom, Julie called a few times, and I can actually make out what he is saying—this at a distance from the receiver of Mom's now old-fashioned land line.

Joseph C. Polacco

It seemed that Mom, the home team, usually came out on top of the "Julie-Vina Debates." However, when Mom would pass the receiver to me, Julie never asked me to take sides; he always asked about my health, and that of my Nancy, kids, and grandkids.

The man *can* cook, however. He even makes his own *salsiccia* (sausage). Of course, Mom always said he used too much salt and oil. I can still see that butter "iceberg" floating in his clam sauce in the skillet. Julie still keeps an eye out for sales on 86th Street, though he can no longer count on Mom to pick up and drop off canned plum tomatoes, a quarter-pound of pine nuts, a tin of Medaglia d'Oro espresso grind, etcetera when she's "in the neighborhood." Beyond Mom's eleven-block walk to the 86th Street emporia, she needed to schlep her two-wheeled cart another two long blocks to Julie's apartment building. She'd say, "What does he think I am? I'm just an old broad, and it's freezing (or hot) out there. If I fall on the ice, goodbye." Then, in the same breath, "You gotta hand it to Julie, he's doing all right for ninety-two, and he has all his marbles."

Combining Florie's grammar and vocabulary with Julie's stories would be a Brooklynese epic poem, with alternate stanzas recited in the unique Brooklyn accents of each. Yes, I believe there are Jewish and Italian variations of the dialect. Of course Mom, the editor, would never agree with Julie's details. So, one Easter Sunday, Nancy and I are at the apartment, and Julie is a guest. I mention *zeppole* and *sfingi*, which unleashes a spirited "discussion" about the difference—classic "Who's on First?" material. Julie says: "Zeppole are fried dough with ricotta filling, like cannoli, and sometimes with a cherry or some other fruit on top. The sfingi have custard filling and powdered sugar."

"Julie, what are you talking about?" says Mom. "The sfingi are stuffed with cannoli cream, and have orange zest and sugar on top."

Then Julie offers, "I remember Alba's Pastry Shop on 18th Avenue, every March and April…" Of course, by now, the battle royal is joined—except that Julie is in general retreat, and sfingi and zeppole changed uniforms several times during the campaign.

I should know the difference between zeppole and sfingi, 'cause these are classic St. Joseph's Day pastries. Mom would send me five bucks and a San Giuseppe card every March 19, *Il Giorno del Mio Onomastico,* which is my name saint's day so I could buy the pastries—not much chance of doing so in Durham, North Carolina or Columbia, Missouri. A sabbatical in the Boston area did provide an outlet at the North End.

Julie's stories keep me enrapt in his redundant biblical style: "So, I get to the door. I open it. I look up, and I hear a noise at the top of the stairs. So, I decided to go upstairs. I'm climbing, and, when I get up there, what do I see? Well, I looked, and..." (Tell me Julie, fercryinoutloud, the suspense is *killing* me!)

Among his several city jobs, Julie was a trolley conductor in his youth, when Brooklyn had trolleys. Indeed, the Brooklyn Dodgers got their name from the Trolley Dodgers. (Got trolleys, Los Angeles, *huh?!* And, while I'm at it, how many *lakes* are there in LA? Why did you not import *water* when you imported the Minneapolis *Lakers*? Too late now.) Julie's trolley navigated all areas, from congested streets to tall-grass marshy fields—much of Bensonhurst is filled-in marshland; *che peccato* (what a pity!) "I gotta make this sharp turn, and cars know to stay outta my way, but this wise guy won't move, and boom, body damage. He had some case against the city." Linguistic sidebar: He had *soooome* case—drawn out, like "He had *no* case, what a *chooch*"—in "high Italian," *ciuccio,* or jackass.

As a kid, I was just another *guaglione,* a ragamuffin kid of the 'hood. *Guaglione* sounds like why-OH, as in, "Why-OH, kay see-deech?" *Guaglione, che si dice?* or "Hey kiddo, whaddya say?" This guaglione recalls taking the West End line the three stops to Coney Island, and a few times seeing Julie working for NYC Transit. He seemed like an Italian Paul Bunyan. He made me feel *okay* for leaving Bensonhurst to go to college. He was great to my kids. I grew in his esteem, became a mensch, as a support for Mom through her difficult times with my stepfather especially at the end of his life, and then again later with her recurrent cancer.

During WWII, Julie was stationed in Natal, Brazil—the only person I know who did that—"I liked it; people were friendly, but a shot of whisky cost fifty cents." Julie was *very* fortunate, and he owes his good luck to *his* mom. "I was born in a little village in Abruzzi, in 1920. My father was in the Italian army during WWI. My mother didn't like what was happening after the war" under Il Duce, Benito Mussolini, and feared for her three sons. Julie's mom encouraged her husband to emigrate to America. After returning to the old country a couple of times, Julie's dad finally settled for good in Brooklyn, with his whole family—Mario, Eddie, kid bro' Giulio, and two sisters. But, Benito had a long arm, and Italians in Brooklyn had to evade it, not just the black hand of local warlords. In Bensonhurst, Julie attended a few meetings run by Mussolini's representatives. The kids were given uniforms, sang patriotic songs, and were promised a free trip to Italy, and thence to Africa to take part in Il Duce's glorious restoration of Imperial Rome. Julie didn't buy into it, but "A good buddy of mine went over, and I never heard from him again."

I don't want to paint a picture of Brooklyn as an extension of the "old country" as embodied by Julie. He and Tootsie made an annual pilgrimage to the Grand Ole Opry. They loved country music. Julie's jeans were held up with a handsome leather belt and cowboy buckle. Julie and Tootsie made friends with other fans from the Southland. South Brooklyn to Southland—what a country.

Watching Julie receive Mom's vitriol—lovingly administered like castor oil—he seemed so mollified, and his retorts were equal parts gruff, tender, and ineffectual. He was Mom's great sparring partner, and each got stronger from their encounters. I saw his strength when I arrived in Brooklyn on the eve of Mom's scheduled lumpectomy. It appeared that she was being swallowed by New York's bureaucratic medical morass—miscommunications and lost messages were about to scotch the surgery. She had to navigate that system, relying on public transportation to various treatment venues. While Mom never learned to drive, Julie's eyesight now precluded it. So, Julie was no longer Mom's escort, and his instructions over the phone were clear and commanding, telling me to take no guff from intermediaries, demand to speak with people in charge, and to force the issue, as a Brooklyn son should. She did have the surgery, endured seven consecutive weeks of daily radiation sessions on her own, and spent the next seven years "cancer-free." Alas, the magic of seven had a time limit.

In mid-2015, I chatted with Julie on the phone. His eyesight problems were now keeping him mostly house-bound. I *know* Mom would have served as his guide-dog on many occasions. Working together in the kitchen? Well, friendship goes only so far.

I quote Julie verbatim: "When I'm on 86th Street, I say 'Vina, where are you?' She had an effect on people—they came to her. If she had a different husband, her house would be like Mary Napolitano's—always full of people."

That may have been the last time we chatted over the phone. A few months later, Julie entered a nursing home, and he passed at the very end of 2015. He lived ninety-five full years.

Photo courtesy Toni Caggiano

Julie, Vina and the Adams at a family gathering.
Front five participants, counterclockwise from left: Tootsie de Ramo, Vina, Georgette Adams, Julie de Ramo, Arthur Adams, 1998; Good-looking lady, left background: Armida, Toni Caggiano's sister.

Joseph C. Polacco

3. Musical Interlude

Music was always a part of Vina's life, and it very much extended to one of her two kids—younger bro' Michael. Mom connected with music at all levels and all genres. This musical interlude takes us from Bensonhurst to Madrid, from the Moulin Rouge to the Bensonhurst Holy Family Home. Julie's Grand Ole Opry and 86th Street music are part of the passing landscape.

Some may recall Shelton Brooks' "The Darktown Strutters' Ball:" "I'll be down to get you in a taxi, honey. You'd better be ready around half past eight; now baby, don't be late…" There was a more "ethnic" version—"I'll be down to get you in a *pushcart*, honey." Pushcarts were code for the Lower East Side, where Mom's two older brothers were born. The Lower East Side was Chinatown, Delancey Street, and, of course, Little Italy.

Lou Monte had a southern Italian dialect version of the "Strutters' Ball," and Mom did a great rendition. As a volunteer in the Holy Family Home, she used to sing a duet of it with an *old fazool* resident—precious. You will note, dear and appreciated reader, that I tend to use Italian-Americanisms throughout my reminiscences. That dormant language virus was awakened by my frequent trips to the "old country" during Mom's struggles. Okay, *fazool*? Every Italian kid knew of *Pasta Fazool*, a hearty dish of *pasta con fagioli* (beans and macaroni). Somehow, we called older Italians, the ones with the accents, "old beans" or "old fazools." We may have liked to say fazool 'cause it started with F and ended with "ool," and rhymed with a curse that translated as "Go sodomize yourself." Or, less colorfully, Brooklynese may have elided "fossil" to "fazool." Alas, there is no Royal Academy of the Brooklyn Language to rule on this. *Royal* Academy? Why not? Brooklyn is the County of Kings.

Mom was also pretty good with Eduardo di Capua's "Eh Marie, Eh Marie," popularized by, among others, Louie Prima and Lou Monte. Mom's singing activities were in line with her being the unofficial entertainment chairlady of the Holy Family Home. She was also the chief seamstress—after all, what is an opera or musical without ostentatious costumes? She made the costumes for the famous Moulin Rouge can-can. Costumes by Vina were complete, so that the finale's showy backward bow demonstrated tastefully ornate, embroidered, bloomer-festooned derrieres that belonged to the volunteers, Mom included. This awakened even the most moribund residents. Oh yeah, Mom did a fine tarantella as well.

Mom's musicality ranged from the prosaic to operatic poetry. I was always amazed at how she was able to keep opera in her life, because we were not the family to traipse to the Met. We lived in three small rooms in back of our linoleum/carpet store on the famous 86th Street, the "Casbah" of open-air markets and small family businesses, all graced with shade from the West End El. My brother and I would sit in front of the store girl watching—especially rewarding in the summer, when the West End El disgorged people returning either from Coney Island or from Manhattan jobs. Stepdad quietly ogled—he not one to voice comments about the young ladies. But, he did not refrain from caustic, intentionally audible remarks about the passing characters. He had a way of casually insulting the Italians in Yiddish and the Jews in Italian—equal opportunity practiced to an art. He slipped these invectives, with a straight face, in the middle of face-to-face conversation. Of course, in keeping with the musical theme, Stepdad did many renditions of "Mala Femmina" ("Evil/Bad Woman" by Totò) from his perch in front of the store; see below. I am sure the ladies saw the irony of that song, a favorite of many males in the 'hood.

More 86th Street and music: Hypochondriac Abe was one of the daily passing characters. "What do I know? I just schlep haberdashery!" We all called him *Healthy*, a nickname coined by stepfather. Abe was deeper than a door-to-door peddler. For example, he loved the opera, and would frequent the Brooklyn Academy of Music. Back in the day, I am sure the BAM was an oxymoron to much of America. Healthy and Mom would occasionally sing a duet to an aria or two—Healthy with a look of ecstasy on his face. I recall their duets in front of the store. When I left home for college and grad school, it was difficult for me to buy my underwear in JC Penney or Sears. And it was difficult for Mom to escape to an opera, a *real* opera, in those days.

Healthy may have had a further cosmic connection to our musical lives. My Argentinian colleague, Ariel Goldraij, informed me that *polaco* meant precisely a Jewish door-to-door peddler in Argentina. Ariel helped further to weave this musical net by telling my brother of his love for the music of the Argentine, Astor Piazzola—"out of the box" tango composer and player of the *bandoneón* (modified accordion). Michael and Ariel connected because Piazzola was already one of my brother's musical heroes.

A couple of years after Mom was widowed, she got to see a whole opera in a truly a beautiful world-class venue. During my sabbatical in Spain in 2000, she and my kids visited over Christmas, and I was able to cop a couple of ducats to Verdi's *Il Trovatore* at Madrid's Teatro Real. However, our entrance was Brooklyn all the way. We took the subway (Metro) from my working-class neighborhood, and she entered El Teatro in an elegant dress she made herself, carrying her own libretto. She had to be the only person, *ever*, to bring to the Teatro Real a libretto from the New Utrecht branch of the Brooklyn Public Library. She was thrilled by the performance, but not by the crowd, which she considered boorish (not the word she used). And, back in Bensonhurst, she dutifully returned the libretto, and on time.

Opera in Bensonhurst could be a selection of arias at the confraternity hall of the neighborhood St. Mary's parish, a street duet with Healthy, old recordings of revered Neapolitan soprano Enrico Caruso, PBS TV/radio shows, or even a very well-planned surprise party in the 'hood. Mom planned Stepdad's seventy-fifth surprise birthday party for years, scrimping and saving, doing seamstress jobs at home, etcetera. She pulled it off. It was at Scarola, a Bensonhurst restaurant where waiters/waitresses were aspiring opera singers. One was the owner's son.

What a night! Stepdad was cranky at the beginning. "Why do I have to take pictures for my niece's wedding shower?" he moaned in the back seat of our car on the way to the restaurant. But, after the initial shock, he had a fantastic time. I still have visions of him dancing in all his finery—yes, he always dressed to the nines, even as a party photographer. The operatic pieces by the service staff were beautiful and poignant. I wished I could sign them to contracts on the spot. The party? Well, we were *all* there. Don't know how Mom did it—the finances, the secrecy, the arrangements, the pretexts for our all being in Brooklyn at that time. While Stepdad had a grand time, he did tease his Vina about being "sneaky."

I suppose Mom's musicality was handed down to kid bro' Michael. We both loved Elvis and Johnny Cash, even before their "coming out" on *The Ed Sullivan Show*. Michael very much took to country and western. He perfected his twang, and he learned the Elvis hip swivels. Amazing to me, he taught himself the guitar. And, I am not sure that he ever learned to read music—he composes to someone who writes it down. Indeed, there was a cowboy yearning for expression inside this ragamuffin Italian street kid. And today Michael (Polacco, Grandi, Grandé—your choice) performs out in Arizona where he and his wife Diane own a horse ranch: *Amber Hills Arabians*, featuring Revelry, Top Ten Stallion and stand Arabian Sire of Significance. But, the locals dig his Brooklyn sagas, and some of them are true. In Michael's musical prime he shared long tours with John Lee Hooker, Canned Heat, and Bedford-Stuyvesant native, Richie Havens. He had shorter stints with others.

So, back to Bensonhurst—as the human caravans of our youth trudged along 86th Street, they sometimes had to part into separate currents around Michael, with his guitar, hip gyrations, and Scotch tape-enhanced Elvis sneer. Understand, 86th Street was the Wall Street of Bensonhurst mercantilism, but nothing was really awry.

So, Vina, your kid is out front making a spectacle of himself. Her face said that he was doing what he loved, *near home*, not hanging at the waterfront with the likes of "Rampers" Jimmy Emma or Sammy "the Bull" Gravano.

In the old days, 86th Street did quiet down on Sunday evenings—it *never* does now—when some a capella groups would take advantage of the unique acoustics of the West End El and its steel support girders. The El structure, however, was not so much a *capella* (chapel), but more of a *cattedrale* (cathedral). I wonder if Dion and the Belmonts sang under an El in the Bronx. Whatever, Michael and I were each a "West End El Niño."

I picture those 86th Street scenes, and music arises, *alla mode di* Dino De Laurentiis: *Vide'o mare quant'è bello; spira tantu sentimentooooooo* (Look at the sea, oh how beautiful; it inspires so many emotions). These Neapolitan dialect lyrics are from "Torna a Surriento," or "Return to Sorrento," by Ernesto De Curtis, and Stepdad often spouted them whilst sitting in front of the store, his back to Gravesend Bay. "Torna a Surriento" was part of his medley. And, as mentioned above, another important component was "Mala Femmina," popularized by Jimmy Roselli. Stepdad could never understand why Jimmy did not supplant Frank Sinatra. Roselli died in 2011, at age eighty-five. *Mannaggia* (dammit), time goes on. I see a parallel between the Sinatra-Roselli and Enrico Caruso-Mario Lanza axes. Roselli was born in Hoboken, NJ, five doors down from Sinatra, who was ten years his senior. According to the Mario Lanza Institute and Museum: "The greatest of all tenors, Enrico Caruso, passed away on August 2, 1921, and on January 31, 1921 in the heart of South Philadelphia, Alfredo Arnold Cocozza (Mario Lanza), the son of Italian immigrants, was born at 636 Christian Street." So, Lanza was not born on the day that Caruso died, as I was always told, but close enough—same year, at least.

Neither Roselli nor Lanza reached the heights of his respective idol.

This chapter is closing out like the fadeout of the Beatles' "Hey Jude." Let it be said here that Mom had a *great* voice, and that she could never understand why I sang like a bullfrog. Also, for the record: My own Nonna Nunziatina, Mom's mom, was virtually deaf, but she *could* hear those scratchy recordings of fellow Napoletano, Caruso.

Polaroid Photo courtesy Polacco family archives

Brother Michael serenading Nonna Nunziatina in the kitchen in the back of our store, early 1960s. *A Nonna* may have humored Michael on occasion.

4. Large Mary and the Little Butterfly

She was larger than life. She was also large, and I apologize to her beautiful daughters for the sobriquet "Mary Fat," but they knew. Mary asked my two-year-old daughter, "Do you know who I am?" and the wide-eyed innocent answer, "You're Mary Fat," was both embarrassing and disarming. Mary, you see, loved children—all children. Her grandkids, nieces and nephews, and neighborhood kids all knew they had to pay with a pint of cheek blood, because Mary had to pinch them. "Come here, so I can eat you alive!" Mary regaled them all with love, but the treats were the real payoff.

On the south side of 86th Street, on the block bordered by 21st Avenue and Bay 26th Street (for the GPS-enabled), lived a concentration of incredible ladies—Large Mary Napolitano, Jeanie (Gruff but Gracious) Gallo, Georgette Seminara Adams, and her aunts, Rose and Mary Seminara. Some time after the passing of Large Mary, these ladies formed a Bible study group that also included Mary's daughter Toni, Florie Ehrlich, and Mom. Many Mary stories are epic, if not biblical, and they are legion and were often exchanged at the Bible Study.

Mary had show biz in her blood. Her face was angelic, and I was told she was a beauty in her youth. Indeed, to me, she radiated beauty. Her uncle, her father's brother, was the famous-for-his-time "*Farfariello.*" The Little Butterfly, Eduardo Migliaccio was a mainstay of immigrant Italian theatre. Yes, in addition to the Yiddish theatre, there was a not-as-well-known Italian one, and doubtless others in the Lower East Side. Bob Hope honored Farfariello. Farfariello based some of his skits on real-life Migliaccio family escapades. The Little Butterfly's comedy was slapstick, and he had to project his voice, often in a falsetto, over the whole raucous audience. Mary also had a booming voice, and she was an extra in some of her uncle's skits. I remember her narrating to Mom and me a funeral story, a true story, in which the black-clad professional mourners would wail, "Who's going to cook the *fish*?!" They wailed, and Mary boomed the retelling. I won't even try to write the lines in the dialect Mary used.

Mary loved Broadway. But, of course, it was in her blood. Mom told me at least three times about their taking a car service to see a show. The driver shows up and sees three ladies. Two are petite Mom and diminutive Carrie, the mother-in-law of Mary's daughter Armida. Carrie lived with Mary. The third lady is Large Mary, and the driver is horrified. He tries to drive away, but they convince him to make the trip. I would wager he avoided the old cobblestoned West Side Highway. Après-theater, they try to hail a cab, to no avail. Finally, Mary hides, they grab a cab, and then Mary appears. Same scenario. But Mary, sitting in the front seat, charms the cabbie and, after landing safely in Bensonhurst, Mom gets out and Mary and Carrie invite the driver for a frappe at Hinsch's Greek Diner. Yes, I *know*, Hinsch's is not a Greek name, but in Brooklyn most diners are/were Greek-owned. Now, mind you, Hinsch's is on 5th Avenue just off 86th Street, fully seventeen *big* blocks from Mary's house, and Mary's husband Jimmy has no idea of the whereabouts of Mary (and Carrie). Ahh, being married to a starlet has its drawbacks.

Not too much of a surprise that Mom connected with Mary—for one thing, they both had generous hearts. One Saturday morning, Mom and dear friend Bianca were returning from errands, and they decided to drop in on Mary. Remember, this was the Bensonhurst of old—dropping in, unannounced, was *expected*, and the folks "passed over" knew of the offense. So, Mom and Bianca spot a guy hiding behind a tree on Bay 26th Street, just as Mary's husband Jimmy is leaving to walk the dog. Soon after, the mystery man enters, and Mary proceeds to supply him, hurriedly, with grated cheese, cans of imported tomatoes (*pomodori pelati*), and various other items. The mystery man was Carl, the husband of Flavia, daughter of Farfariello. Mary was an easy touch, and hated to see cousin Flavia go through tough times. Mom and Bianca were also charitable ladies, but they scolded Mary for being so devious. Mom relayed this story to Toni, who later told me, "Well, that was my mom, a giver, and sad to say, there were takers." My stepdad tried to intervene on Mom's generosity, 'cause he looked at the world as takers. And I think Jimmy—Toni's stepdad, from the old country, and with a suspicious facial scar—felt the same way. Yes, experience proved them right on a few occasions, but better to suffer the takers, while helping the truly needy, than not help at all. I, Joe Polacco, said that, and Mom agrees, even now.

Okay, I am using terms like "angelic" and "generous" and "charitable" to describe my mom, everyone's Aunt Vina. But, she also had immigrant peasant toughness. One hazy, opressively hot summer afternoon of particularly bad quality air—the kind that used to hurt your chest on deep inhalation—I was hanging in front of the linoleum store, and the upstairs lady comes down, trying to escape the heat. There was bad blood between the upstairs lady and Mom. (At the time, I'm not sure we owned the two-story building; the upstairs lady was either our tenant or neighbor, but in any case, we still lived in back of the store.) The upstairs lady starts to bad-mouth Mom to Stepdad Lou. To his credit, he says, "You can't shine her shoes." Things get nasty, and I remember the upstairs lady saying, "Vina cooks with a lot of grease; that's why your kids have pimples!"

Mom is now coming home, drudging off the West End after a day in a hot garment union (sweat) shop, and she gets wind of the last comment. "Oh, I give my kids pimples?" One thing leads to another, and then a tremendous *fight*—I mean a no-holds-barred *lady fight*—breaks out. Mom proceeds to kick the lady's butt, and is wiping the hard mean sidewalk with her. Three patrol cars show up; the guys inside were beat cops, and were known, so this was more community relations than law enforcement. The whole scene was more entertaining to the passersby than my bro's Elvis renditions. Man, I saw a woman capable of turning her love and caring into animal ferocity against someone who would slam her kids and the care she provided them.

I never asked Mom about that fight, and I am sure she would have been very embarrassed even to acknowledge it. Happily, my three hours of recordings of her during her last six months were filled with non-violent stories, recipes, and laughs.

Mary Fat and Aunt Vina were just two of the very large women in the 'hood. Taking care of others was what the 'hood did. There were street folks who were "developmentally challenged," and they always seemed to find food and support and shelter. They were part of the ecosystem. One of my bro's friends, upon seeing a down-and-outer slurping a bowl of hot soup in back of our store, came out with, "What *is* dis, da Brooklyn Rescue Mission?" This was mentioned in the Introduction, but it bears repeating: *Brooklyn Rescue Mission* was the name of my brother's first CD.

I do not want to paint a picture of "My Sainted Mother." *All* Italian mothers are sainted—the "mala femmina" referred to *moglie* (wives) or *innamorate* (girlfriends). And *all* mothers, including Mary and Vina, would drop their wings at times, and recognize human imperfection. For instance, some of the friends my brother and I brought home were *scassigazzi*, and they were probably better than the *ruffiani*. The former were just "ballbusters," but the latter, worse—two-faced sycophants, a little bit like Eddie Haskell. Ballbuster is a loose translation—scassigazzo referred to a more singular aspect of male anatomy. But even these deviant characters received Mom's attention, though she could see through them. The same goes for Large Mary.

Finally, I cannot close a chapter on Large Mary without a mention of her three beautiful daughters, Triple A-rated: Amelia, Armida, and especially the youngest, Antonina (Toni Caggiano). They were great supporters of Mom, as well as recipients of her support. Toni was also a regular at the famous Bay 26th Street Bible Study. And now, Toni's three daughters have bestowed eight beautiful grandchildren upon her. Toni carries on the tradition of strong and loving Brooklyn women, and I won't call her a "flat leaver" for moving to Jersey.

This from Toni:

> One year after my mom passed when we lived in Brooklyn, I had to have a birthmark removed from my back. I was recommended to a doctor in Manhattan. I went with my husband Vinny, and was told to return in two weeks to have the stitches removed. The first available appointment was 7:15 a.m. My husband worked in New Jersey, so I thought I'd go myself and not have him take off work again. At 6:15 a.m. my doorbell rang, and there was Aunt Vina. She had walked from her house at 77th Street to mine on West 3rd Street (a considerable walk) to go with me, because she did not want me to be alone—because I didn't have my mom. That was her, always going the extra mile. We made a little day of it, and because of her, I looked at Manhattan in a different light. She made me notice the tops of buildings, and she showed me the Garment Center statue of the seamstress at the sewing machine.
>
> Twenty years later, she had to go to her primary doc and bring her mammogram—not an easy feat since the mammo was at 94th Street and the Health Insurance Plan Center was at 67th Street and 10th Avenue [both in Brooklyn]. I surprised her, picking up the mammo and taking her to the doc. She was so grateful. She never asked for favors, but she could thank you for giving her one.

But wait! There is more from Toni:

> Aunt Vina loved a bargain. My niece was getting married, and [daughter] Cara was her flower girl. My niece had a picture of a dress she wanted Cara to wear. It had a layer of lace on the bottom of the hem. This was also Cara's first communion time, and without benefit of a pattern, Vina made the dress with a detachable lace hem that we removed for her first communion. The entire cost of the fabric was twelve dollars, and she wore the dress twice. She looked beautiful, and no one had the same dress. Of course we did lunch after the fabric store, at the now-famous half sandwich shop on 18th Avenue.
>
> All in all, it was always a great day when I was with her—she was always good company and great fun. She filled a big void in my life, with her old world wisdom, cheerfulness, and caring. She was a blessing in my life. I hope you, Joe, get comfort in knowing how loved she was. Boy do I miss her.

So, Aunt Vina was big enough to fill, at least partially, the void left by Large Mary. And, I add that Toni was instrumental in getting the Holy Family Home to memorialize Aunt Vina's contributions.

Joseph C. Polacco

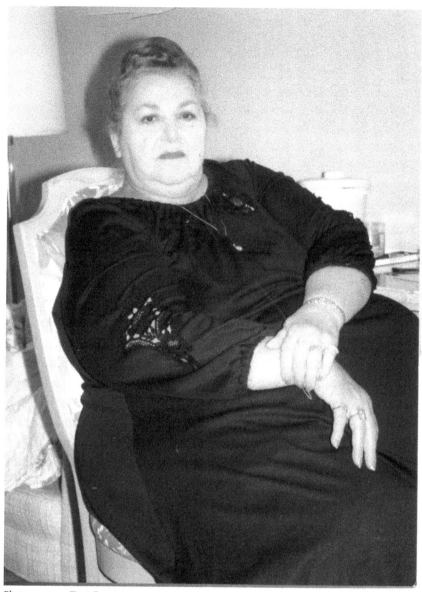

Photo courtesy Toni Caggiano

Large Mary, in a pensive pose.

5. Sandy, Fish, and the *Maloik*

Sandy Irrera supported and extended Mom's missions of mercy, while also aiding Mom, especially in her dealings with recurrent cancer. This was fitting because Mom and Sandy met at an American Cancer Society Relay for Life fundraiser during the seven years that Mom was "cancer-free." Sandy's real name is Santa, and though the reader might be tempted to picture her as saintly, she is more of an earthy dynamo—an angel hell-bent on helping the less fortunate. She deserved to be called Mom's guardian angel.

While Sandy and Mom worked to help the unfortunate, they managed to frustrate and aggravate each other, but with a lot of laughs. Perhaps Sandy, thirty-five years younger, was the daughter Mom never had, and Mom probably filled the void left by Sandy's loss of her mom at a very young age. Or, they just made an energetic pair of kooky ladies.

When I think of Sandy, I think of charity in overdrive, seafood (any fish), and the *malocchio*, or evil eye. Before I explain, before the reader tries to make connections, some background:

Mom loved Sandy, but Mom also loved saving money—a life-long trait, probably born of her depression-era childhood with three siblings and a single, deaf immigrant mom who spoke little English. Mom's dad, a milliner, made hats of his own design. Clients, I was told, were from Broadway and films. At the cusp of the Great

Depression, Charles—Calógero, I believe—ran off to California with a young actress client. Sandy, was of a later generation, hence more profligate, and at times this trait exasperated Mom. But, Sandy never really knew the depression, nor did I, though I still try to emulate Mom's thriftiness and her custom of holding food sacred. Several times Mom told me that her mother, my Nonna Nunziatina, actually kissed food goodbye that she *had* to throw away.

Though Mom always loved to eat, her frugal nature meant that she did not go out much. However, a bargain is a bargain, and it could be had at a diner-deli on 18th Avenue and sixty-something street— worth the walk from Mom's place on 21st Avenue and 77th Street. This was the "famous half-sandwich shop" that Toni Caggiano mentioned in the previous chapter. The place had a perpetual special: half sandwich of pastrami or corned beef, cup of soup, and a drink—Mom and I always went for seltzer with a lemon slice. All this for $4.99, *and* of course, half of a bracing kosher dill pickle cut length-wise.

Mom took Sandy there once.

To set the scene: The sandwich was packed New York deli style—the meat could be redistributed into a whole sandwich in mid-America. It was on good rye or pumpernickel, and especially great when dripping with mensch mustard. The hearty soup was home-made: split pea, barley and beef, for example. The service was Brooklyn friendly ("whaddya havin' sweetie?"), and the clientele was, well, Bensonhurst. A nearby lawyer ate there daily—hey, a bargain is indeed a bargain. And a lonely soul virtually lived there. They *let* him stay—the 'hood has a heart.

So, after lunch, Sandy "expletived" all about how hungry she still was: "What the hell *is* this? Are you crazy?" Mom and Sandy went into uncontrollable laughing fits: conniptions. I think they needed another $4.99 round—two for $8.99? You will see "conniptions" mentioned elsewhere in this narrative. Some may associate this with rage or anger, but I prefer happy hysteria.

Sandy's people are from Sciacca. In Bensonhurst back in the day it was not enough to say you were Italian, not even Sicilian, Neapolitan,

Romano, etcetera; you also had to indicate the *paese*—the village or environs. Sciacca is a Sicilian town of fishermen, and many, or most, fish stores in Brooklyn were run by *gli sciacchitani* (sounds like "e shock-ee-DON"). Sandy, of course, served "fish" often at home, which really meant shellfish—shrimp, clams, mussels, octopus (*polpo*—in dialect, "ee BOOP"), *calamari* (squid), etcetera. Some of Sandy's family was in the fish business. All stores in the "bizzhi-*ness*" featured live eels, great aromas, and all that *frutti di mare*. I loved to go to fish places, especially around the holidays. Most were on 18th Avenue, but there was always a store within walking distance. In the 'hood, you bought a fish and, if you wanted, they would fillet it for you and give you the bones to make a broth—no extra charge. Watching those guys work was part of the culinary experience.

In the *old* "old days," fish stores had a dried, salted codfish hanging over the portal—nailed to it actually, in all kinds of weather, all year round, until it was taken down for the holidays, rehydrated, and baked with tomatoes, onions, and potatoes—quite good. Of course, they sold more than this one "masthead" specimen. This was dried *bacalá*, or *stoccafisso,* an Italianization of "stock fish," not to be confused with fish stock. Mom said "*stocca-baccalà.*" Cod comes from cold waters; partial credit goes to the Portuguese—navigators, fishermen, and merchants—for making it so popular in Italy, Spain, Brazil, and the Caribbean. I picked up some salted cod in Spain, soaked it with several water changes, and cooked it according to Mom's recipe. The first bite sucked out half my blood volume— you *really* have to soak out the salt. In cold, dry climates, such as Norway's, no need for salt.

Another 'hood seafood treat was *scungilli,* or conchs. They are great boiled, diced, and served in a fresh seafood salad with bitter green olives, celery, octopus tentacle sections, and the assorted dislodged sucker. I am forgetting other ingredients, and this recipe, I am afraid, is gone with Mom. Scungilli is also a term for a "gavoon," a slow greenhorn from the other side. "Gavoon" is how the dialect form of *cafone* (peasant) sounded to me. Gavoon is a useful word; I even heard Dom DeLuise use it on TV. I never knew how much

I appreciated bacalá, *vongole* (cherrystone clams), scungilli, crab, etcetera, until I made my way to the mid-American "fish sticks." Though I hasten to add that fishing can be a cult in Missouri.

Linguistic/culinary/cultural side trip: I do not want to denigrate Missouri's fish culture—Missouri is almost a coastal inland state; within its borders are the confluence of the Missouri and Mississippi Rivers, many springs, spring-fed clear rivers, lakes, and fishing holes. So fishing is a passion to many Missourians, and a favorite is the "crappie," pronounced croppie—careful with your pronunciation, out-of-towners. And, I should mention our own paddle fish; a living fossil and a source of Missouri caviar.

While I commuted between Missouri and Brooklyn, older generations of Italians tended to commute between New York and the old country, though the trip back often convinced them the right choice was having gone to *Mannaggia'merica* (damn America) in the first place. Sandy's uncle traveled back to Sciacca; however, he married and stayed there. When he passed, his Sicilian widow became the beneficiary of an American account of some kind. How to communicate with this woman? Mom was the designated "interlocutor." She spoke some "high Italian" (Toscano), but was better at the dialects of Naples, Bari, and Palermo (Belmonte Mezzagno)—the latter picked up from my stepdad's extended family. Mom had to engage in a "dialectic" to convince "La Signora Vedova" to sign the papers and forward the death certificate to Brooklyn. Imagine doing this over the phone, and dealing with the normal Sicilian undercurrents of mistrust. We Americans can't really appreciate dealing with millennia of clashing cultures, plots, wars, invasions, shifting alliances, and *omertà* (code of silence). Just look at us in the Middle East; Mom might have helped. By the way, Mom succeeded, convincing *A Signora* to sign the paper and forward it to Brooklyn.

Sandy's husband Tommy grew up in the Little Italy of Martin Scorsese. In those days, many residents were not catering to tourists, but were more motivated to avoid getting "whacked." Tommy is an engineer, and he and Sandy have two successful daughters. I have said more than once that Tommy is a prince, but he's really more like a saint, 'cause the former sounds Machiavellian. Tommy is San Tommaso to Sandy's Santa, and is completely behind Sandy's charity work—as in he can't keep up, but he is *sooo* forbearing. Sandy's specialty is making gift baskets to be auctioned at fund-raisers. She "puts the squeeze" on local businesses, and stocks the baskets well. And, the baskets usually occupy a whole room at the Irrera home. Tommy accepts this—as in "Grant me the serenity to accept the things I cannot change."

Mom, and Sandy before her, were recognized as "Women of the Year" by New York State Senator Marty Golden, representing Brooklyn's 22nd District, which is comprised of several neighborhoods. In March of 2011, I came in from Missouri for the evening event honoring Mom and the other winners. Indeed, the other women were very deserving, but it seemed to me that they did their good deeds as part of their professional duties—school principals, guidance counselors, et al. But Mom and Sandy were "free agents." Bless Sandy for calling Mom to Senator Golden's attention. Mom was definitely not into self-promotion, or resumé building, as David Brooks might say.

Mom and Sandy both believed in the malocchio. The evil eye is also "maloik" in the 'hood. You get it when someone "overlooks" you, expressing grudging congratulations or a compliment, but really dying of jealousy and resentment—new house, new car, beautiful grandchild—and thinking, "Yeah, she should get a hernia for her troubles." Hence, be very discreet about bragging; as I say elsewhere, Mom hated to brag about her kids or grandkids for this very reason. She was concerned for her kin, and not so much for herself.

There was a time when Sandy did not believe in the maloik, but her husband Tommy did, as did his mom, of course. Sandy became a believer when she endured five days of a low-grade headache—one that Tylenol, aspirin, etcetera could not help. Her mother-in-law checked her out by placing a saucer of olive oil on Sandy's forehead as she reclined. Sandy's mother-in-law added water to the oil, and when it broke up into separate droplets, she screamed, "You have it!"

They flushed the mixture as rapidly as possible; happily, plumbing is not susceptible to the maloik—but who knows? They repeated the oil and water test, and again the same result. Upon the third try, the water droplet did not disperse, and Sandy was declared "cured" or freed of the maloik. Her headache immediately went away, and all the saints were thanked.

To be able to deal with the malocchio, according to Sandy, involves reciting a special prayer, in Italian, in front of a church on Christmas Eve. Sandy does not know Sciacchitano, but her sister Vivian does, and so could become a practitioner. (*Curandera* in Spanish and English in the southwestern United States. The Italian *Strega*, or witch, is probably too strong, the latter more likely to cast the malocchio on the unsuspecting.)

Another means of warding off the malocchio is to wear the "little horn," or *cornetto*. The cornetto looks like a golden chili pepper, and I have seen it often in Bensonhurst, a pendant on hairy-chested "goombahs." GoomBAH is now part of American popular culture, thank you Hollywood—and HBO's *The Sopranos*. It is derived from *compare*—not only the religious godfather but also countryman—and based on the Neapolitan form, *cumpà*. The female equivalent, *comare*, is "goomAH-dey." The goombahs may be "inoculated," but to me they looked like carriers. When my daughter came on the scene, over forty years ago, a charming elderly guy in the 'hood told Mom to pick up the "horn" in Little Italy—he made the horn sign with his index finger and pinky—'cause she was sure to attract the malocchio. However, Sandy's kin had another pre-emptive measure: the grandma of her daughter's boyfriend gave her a red ribbon to wear in her bra to ward off the "eye," as did Sandy's grandma on her own wedding day. I keep on having to ablate the image of an accessorized training bra.

Finally, I don't want to convey an assertion that the maloik is an Italian invention; it is probably universal. I lived in both Colombia and Brazil, and folks feared the *mal de ojo* in the former, and the *mal-olhado/olho gordo* in the latter. In both places, the fusion of African and Catholic rites has engendered a rich tradition, and trade, in repellants and cures. Even Maimonides railed against belief in "the eye."

Sandy and Mom with some cancer survivors. Sandy is second from left, top row, and Mom, second from right, bottom row. September 2012.

Presentation of Women of Year award by New York State Senator Marty Golden, March 2011.

Joseph C. Polacco

6. Georgette, La Vucciria, and La Moda

No story about Georgette Adams is complete without including her never-married aunts, Mary and Rose, ninety-six, and one-hundred-one years old as I write this. "Spinster" is, yes, a pejorative, but if a pair of unmarried sisters deserves to wear the title as an honorific, it is Mary and Rose. They live together by their lonesome in a large wood-frame house, and their backyard is just "katty korner" from where Georgette's backyard *was*. Georgette's house *used to be* on 21st Avenue, two houses south of commercial 86th Street, but seemingly in a different, more rural world—rural by Bensonhurst standards. In the not-so-old days, sweet Georgette would call in on her aunts daily. While Mary was perfectly able to engage in the Olympic event of shopping on 86th Street, Georgette often shopped for the sisters, and ministered to them in other ways.

I need to digress about 86th Street, the "Casbah" so important in the life of Mom and of those she touched. The north side of the long block between Bay Parkway (22nd Avenue) and 23rd Avenue consists of open-air produce and schlock markets cheek by jowl, most of which have space inside for cash registers, dry goods, and more merchandise/produce. The owners have changed over the years, from Jewish and Italian in the fifties and sixties, to Koreans, Chinese, Egyptians, Arabs, Russians, et al. While Asians have conglomerated neighboring businesses into open-air "supermarkets," at least one Italian family has done the same. Hence, La Vucciria encompasses at least three contiguous properties and on the inside, in addition to Italian favorites such as artichokes and *broccoli di rapa* (robbies), there is a functioning Russian deli counter, tended by white tunic-clad young Russian ladies. You vant smoked fish? You *got* it. *Ochin xharascho! Molto bene! That's Brooklyn.* La Vucciria is aptly named. It means, loosely, "madhouse," and is the title of Renato Guttuso's famous painting of the "palermitano" market, which depicts a scene reminiscent of 86th Street. It's life imitating art, imitating life. A large picture, a mural almost, of *La Vucciria* adorns the Bensonhurst namesake.

Now, fresh produce has always made 86th Street famous, even before fresh produce was cool and co-opted by the young hipsters by the Brooklyn Bridge and DUMBO. DUMBO? Well, almost Disneyesque, but it stands for "Down Under the Manhattan Bridge Overpass." The West End line goes over the Manhattan Bridge—flanked by the Brooklyn Bridge to the south and the Williamsburg Bridge to the north. Back in the day, you were more likely to find bodies by the bridge than the modern, more genteel tourist attractions like picnicking and kayaking.

On 86th Street in Bensonhurst, if you're picking through produce when a bunch of new *carciofi* (artichokes) or string beans is dumped on the stand, you have to fight a gaggle of aggressive ladies (and a few brave, battle-hardened men) on the lookout for the prime specimens. And they also know about positioning, blocking out, and using elbows. Rose Seminara, the elder, when she was in her late eighties—early nineties, was right there. From Georgette: "Your mom was helping my Aunt Rose pick out string beans. They were picking them out *one-by-one*, not by the handful, because Mary would have a fit if Rose came home with spotted or rotten beans." Now, this was a bitterly cold day, mind you, and Rose was putting bony, delicate, yet rapacious fingers on the choice specimens.

When the man came and dumped a new crate of string beans over the old ones, my aunt emptied the already full bag and proceeded to start over, and your mom said, "Enough! Rose, you got to be kidding!"

I heard this story from Mom as well as from Georgette, and I could just see Mom saying: "*Abbastanza! Ma, quando, MAI?!*" Roughly translated, "Enough! When will you be done, NEVER?!" Not even Mom could put her numb fingers through another string bean hunt. Now, if they were for her own table, probably a different story.

Rose, Mary, and Georgette are of the talented and accomplished Seminara clan—Sicilians who belie Hollywood stereotypes. Their numbers include dentists, lawyers and doctors. Aurora Seminara, PhD, was a student of 1998 Nobel Prize winner Ferid Murad. Stephanie Seminara is currently Professor of Medicine at Harvard Medical School. Earlier in her career she was able to master human genetics and genomics to identify a "puberty gene" which she called part of "the pilot light of puberty." Georgette married Arthur Adams, of Canton, Ohio: "I met Art after he came out of the Navy (six years—during Vietnam). He went home for a while, and then came to the big city, New York. We met through a friend."

To me, Arthur has thoroughly demonstrated how the environment can influence the "epigenome," so that he is now a full-blown goombah. Talk about the confluence of the 'hood and rural mid-America: Arthur is now a conductor for the New York Transit Authority, and pilots the West End Express. (Currently the D, but we all know, and use, the *real* name.) As he barreled down 86th Street between the 20th Avenue and Bay Parkway (22nd Avenue) stations, he tooted his horn to his bride, who stood waving at him from her 21st Avenue back porch. Alas, no more. They had to sell a house that was sitting on a large footprint, on which will soon stand a five-story luxury condominium, with stores at ground level and subterranean parking. And so continues gentrification; enough of that.

I should not get too maudlin or hand-wringing, 'cause in the very old days, Brooklyn was a collection of Dutch farming communities, and efforts to stem urbanization bore no fruit. Old Peter Stuyvesant, New York's last Dutch governor (1664), probably did a few roll-overs in his grave over the Bensonhurst of my youth. However, this does not mean that today there are no urban gardens. Indeed, I cultivated tomatoes, Swiss chard (*bietola*, or *scarola*, depending on who you ask), and gogozelle (*cucuzza*, or goo-GOOTZ, in dialect; a long, sinuous light green squash) in the postage stamp of exposed soil behind our three rooms. A Sicilian immigrant, Mr. Spadaro, bought and renovated the house over the back fence. He commandeered neighbors' terrain, and his backyard looked like a rural garden, complete with a grape trellis and fig trees he had to prune and wrap in tar paper to over-winter. He encouraged my "farming," and would often water my plants through the chain-link fence. I was the *farmiol* (farm-eye-OHL, as it sounded to me in dialect). Mrs. Spadaro shared some of her husband's tomato preserves with us each year. It didn't hurt that Mom was extremely good to her. The cover photo captures Mom chatting over the back fence with Lucia (Lucy) Spadaro about grandkids. I am thankful I did not become bipolar living in the linear gradient traced from 86th Street madness, through our store, and home to the Spadaro rural Sicilian plot.

So, Georgette and Arthur's home was a parcel of the "rural residue" of Bensonhurst. Though their house was large, its footprint was less than half of their lot; so, they could grow tomatoes, *basilicó* (basil—bah-zilly-GO in dialect), peppers, etcetera. They even had a chicken—an escapee from a neighbor child's Easter present. The chick crawled through the fence, and Arthur built a roost for her. Over the last few of her eleven years, she just nestled in with the curled-up dog on the back porch.

Georgette sings to my mother many mornings, and prays for her soul and the health of my daughter as well. Mom used to bring her aunts, "the sisters," the Sunday editions of the *Daily News* and *New York Post* and then stay for morning coffee and breakfast, dropping by Georgette's on the way home. I loved that Florie and Georgette got to know each other through their own mothers. I never knew those ladies, but I think that they were part of a vanguard of womanhood looking for expression and fulfillment beyond the familial.

Georgette is a smart cookie, but she is so good that she sometimes crumbles when she should hold fast, at least in my opinion. When I'm tempted to sound off on my professional accomplishments to Georgette and Arthur, I am chastened by the evidence of their strong intellects. For example, Georgette is a master of Sudoku, and Arthur, a master mechanic. Not that they brag—the evidence is all over the house, and Georgette and Arthur are heroes to their three children-in-law. The Italian lineage is now yet another ingredient in the protean Brooklyn minestrone, and their grandkids impart flavors of Haiti, Georgia (the ex-Soviet Republic), and other locales, and it's all good, tasty, and sustaining. Mom was absolutely delirious over Georgette's grandson Quinn.

Georgette also appreciated genius in others. Once, when sewing kitchen curtains,

> Vina asked if she could do it for me. I thanked her and told her that I wanted to do it myself as a project. I was okay with straight seams, but when I needed to make the pleats for the hooks, I couldn't get it right. Sooooo, I waited for Vina to come by, which she always did when on 86th Street, and she proceeded to teach me how to do the pleats—so easy when shown by a master. She supervised me while I did them on my machine, and left it to me to finish.

Georgette then needed to place trim on the kitchen window over the sink to match the curtains.

> Well, after trying several times to get it right, I was ready to throw the whole thing out. Again Vina, without hesitation, came to my rescue. She

took the curtain home, and next day delivered to me the finished curtain complete with the matching trim. They have been on my window ever since. I don't change them, just wash them and put them back up. I love them. It's funny how at the time something like that could seem so insignificant, but now when I look at them, they remind me of her. They remind me how very blessed I was to have Vina in my life.

Mom's creations made it out of the neighborhood, to Manhattan's Upper East Side. Follow the winding plot: Leonard Sillman, Broadway producer/show biz entrepreneur, had "discovered" my brother Michael when he was working on a Pietro D'Agostino & Sons demolition project. After hearing Michael sing and play guitar, he featured Bro' as one of his "New Faces of 1971" in the February 20 issue of *Cue* magazine, page 9:

> MICHAEL POLACCO. I first saw this multifaceted talent on the corner of my street, where a building was being demolished. This young Italian-American was part of the demolition squad. Each day, when work finished at three, this steel-helmeted young man got into his 1956 T-bird and roared down Fifth Avenue. My curiosity got the best of me, and I asked him what he was all about. He worked in demolition during summers to make enough money to finish at Visual Arts, and he didn't know whether to be a camera man, a movie director, or a performer. Then, one day he played the guitar and sang for me. I immediately recognized a potential star. Michael is a brilliant lyricist-composer, and he has warmth and charm which, when he performs, light up any room. He has that marvelous thing called communication. Michael has just finished his first record album, and

is looking for the right distributor. His songs are of today, tomorrow, and sometimes yesteryear.

In the early seventies, Michael helped girlfriend Theo get a job as one of Leonard's assistants. Theo wore some of Mom's creations around the office—cape, shawl, scarf, etcetera—and they caught Leonard's eye. When told they were designed and made by Vina, Michael's mom, Leonard realized he had already complimented Michael on a couple of his shirts, also made by Mom.

Leonard showed some of Vina's creations to his dear friend Elinor S. Gimbel, a scion of the Gimbel family. At the time, Macy's and Gimbel's were the two department store behemoths/leviathans. I use these two descriptors because both are borrowed from the Hebrew: Macy/Gimbel—de "oy" mit da "vey." Leonard and Elinor were practically neighbors, both living in the upper 70s near 5th Avenue. So, Elinor was excited as well, and Michael, Leonard, and Elinor conspired to open some type of boutique in Manhattan. They had gone as far as having brochures and business cards printed. Michael recalls, "They were very fancy and done in pink!" Mom, humble as usual, simply couldn't understand why they'd want her clothes, especially when there were so many other designers in New York City. But indeed they did, and their money talked. It said "Designs by Vina" were just as elegant and beautiful as any, even the designs coming out of France.

To get to the end of this winding story, Mom, meeting fierce resistance at home, gave up this dream. Realistically, this is a "tale of two cities." The Silk Stocking District of the Upper East Side is *not* Bensonhurst. For Mom to open a store in Manhattan, when she lived behind our family's store in Bensonhurst, well, this was a twain not joined, not back in the day anyway (early seventies). But, I can imagine Mom's morale must have sunk when she then reported to the neighborhood "sweat shop" to sew someone else's more pedestrian designs.

Mom met Leonard twice, but never met Elinor. Perhaps if she had—one strong woman of means inspiring a woman of talent and immense inner strength—the outcome may have been different. But we will never know.

Mom's pain over this incident was evident in her sharing it. Georgette remembers:

> Your mom told me of the time she was offered to go to work in Manhattan. Louie put up a fuss. That's all I know. I don't know any details of the story except that she was sorry she did not go, because who knows what that would have led to. She was creative and talented beyond being just good and great. She was superb—a marvel in clothing design.

Toni Caggiano, daughter of Large Mary, has a similar take.

Another anecdote, this from near the end of Mom's life, comes from the artist, Sol Schwartz—a graduate of The High School of Music and Art (now Fiorello LaGuardia High) in New York City and a buddy of my cousins, Rosalie and Jim Mangano. Sol had a bunch of woven woolen "swatches," which his wife was going to make into a sweater for their fifth great-grandchild. Sadly, his wife passed, and the project was passed down, but whoever was in charge was baffled. So, Jim and Rosalie recommended Mom, who put them together into a beautiful little outfit. Sol was gracious enough to write to me. I include his hastily written message for two reasons. First, it is a great example of New York vernacular. Secondly, Sol passed on Christmas day, 2015, five days before Julie's passing, and so, the following is even more precious to me:

> She did a wonderful thing by putting together a sweater my late wife had knitted but died before completing …. for her great-grandchild number five. Your mother not only put the entire sweater together, but made the most beautiful buttonholes

that had not been completed as well. I bless her, and Jim and Rosalie Mangano for having done this. Our fifth great-grandchild is now wearing that sweater.

Sol was so thankful, he offered to pay, but Mom refused. So he gave her an autographed copy of his 2001 book, *Drawing Music: The Tanglewood Sketchbooks* (Tom Cross, Inc.), which features sketches of musicians performing at Tanglewood. I now own that dedicated volume, with lovely, expressive sketches—of the likes of Mstislav Rostropovich and Seiji Ozawa.

So, Sol became part of Mom's circle. Vina could not just deal with people in an impersonal or professional context. They had to be family, and that list includes Tony the Fruit Guy, Sal the Tomato Man, Kim of Kim's Fresh Produce, her hearing aid guy, and Chris Corritore who did her taxes. In most cases, there was an opportunity to make a creation for a new baby in the family.

During tax season I got this from Chris, who still does my taxes.

> Words cannot describe what your mother meant to me. I always think of the smile that she brought to my face when she walked into my office. She really didn't have to do taxes but I made sure to do everything I could to make sure [she got] something back every year—just so she could have a reason to sit with me.
>
> I can only imagine her in her last days suffering but still having the patience, willingness and determination to knit my little girl [Isabella; I remember, Chris] the most beautiful pink sweater I've ever seen. I'll always keep it as a memory.

Mom was not morbid, in spite of the knocks. This "old broad" aged gracefully, and was fond of saying, *"A vecchiaia è na carogna,"* dialect for "old age is a rotting putrid corpse." I forgot the phraseology for the alternative of growing old, thinking it was something like, "Better to smell old than smell dead," but, University of Missouri colleague, Professor Carol Lazzaro-Weis, suggested something more poetic: "*ma per chi non ci arriva è una vergogna!*" Or, "but for those who don't get that far, it's a shame!" (Tante grazie, Professoressa, that's what Mom said!). Georgette, like most, loved Mom's sense of humor:

> I must say that for a woman whose life was not always smooth, she had a lot of humor. While visiting in the hospital with Joe [yours truly] and Phyllis [Florie's niece], we got on the subject of death. We were saying that we are not so good at dealing with death. We were discussing sayings like "God wanted him," or "It was his time," or "She passed on," and when we got to "Only the good die young," Vina said, "What does that mean? That if you live to an old age, you are mean and rotten?" And we laughed and laughed. That was Vina—she always had the punch line. I'll bet she is keeping them hopping in heaven. Miss her a lot.

They also miss Mom in the Holy Family Home (for the elderly and otherwise incapacitated). Toni Caggiano and Georgette went to the HFH to seek out administrators to get permission to hang a dedicatory plaque for Mom. A "second-in-command" was on hand, Denise Daniello, and as Georgette recounts:

> Toni explained that she wanted a plaque in Vina's name. The response, get this: "*Do it.* I knew Vina, a wonderful woman. I was sorry to hear that she died. She did an enormous amount of work here." She was so receptive; Toni couldn't believe it [and] started crying. I don't think Toni expected such a response. Toni asked, "What about the new

Joseph C. Polacco

manager?" Denise said, "I'll deal with him; I'll talk to him. I'll put the plaque in the recreation room, which is where she did a lot of work." Toni started crying again. And so it went.

On May 31, some months later, there was a memorial mass for Mom at the home, coinciding with the mass that celebrates pregnant Mary's visit to her cousin Elizabeth. And after the mass, there was a lovely dedication of the plaque. The food spread had only a little to do with the fantastic turnout. Georgette is convinced that Mom "connived" to make sure that the right person dealt with Toni, and that the traffic on the Verrazzano Bridge from Jersey was light that morning.

If you have stayed with me this far, you will have noticed how intertwined are the lives of Mom, Georgette, Large Mary, Toni, Florie, Phyllis (and Florie's mom, who was also Phyllis' grand aunt), et al.— and the list is abridged for clarity and privacy. The aforementioned happened to share a hallway in a Bensonhurst apartment building, and those bonds have lasted for at least forty years. And, Carrie, Armida's second husband's mother, was also the mother of Tootsie, Julie's late wife. So, Armida and Tootsie were sisters-in-law. If this seems gnarly, you can understand why we Italians are all just "cousins." Mom, however, had all these relationships down pat.

Photo courtesy Georgette Adams

Georgette and Mom at the wedding of
Georgette's niece, Ana Marie, center.

Cara—Toni Caggiano's daughter—in communion dress made by Vina.

Photos courtesy Toni Caggiano

Vina and pregnant Cara at Nancy Adams' wedding (Circa 2007). Mom altered Cara's dress, yet again.

Joseph C. Polacco

7. Sorority of the Strong.

In her later years Mom had several 'circles:' the Kiwanians, the Holy Family staff and residents, her Condo association, Sandy's cancer survivor-support groups, the neighborhood, and the D'Agostino clan. But, I believe that her Bible Study Group was especially notable as a coterie of strong and independent women:

Toni Caggiano was a regular in "our prayer meeting," to which the members brought different traits:

> Rose Seminara (blind faith), Mary Seminara (doubting Thomas), your Mom (extremely knowledgeable bible scholar), Florie (the atheist), Jean Gallo (devil's advocate), Georgette (peace broker), myself (the novice, the sponge trying to take it all in). I walked away from these meetings feeling the main idea was to love one another and share the love. I also felt the presence of my Mom [Mary Napolitano] so many times.
>
> Joe, if your book does nothing else, it will show how your Mom's life mattered, how she gave of herself in so many ways, that her contributions on this earth were unmistakable. But, all these women are unsung heroes.

Amen and thank you, Toni. Among the unsung heroes, I had the least personal interaction with Jean Gallo. Jean lived three houses away from the Seminara sisters, Rose and Mary. A properly placed rectangle covering contiguous 21st Avenue and Bay 26th Street would include the houses of Jean, Georgette, the Seminara sisters, and Mary Napolitano and her daughter Toni, four out of nine houses by my estimate, and the other five were not strangers to them. Who says the big city is "cold?"

I am amazed that Mom became such an integral part of a Bible study that had more gnarly interrelationships than a Texas thicket. For instance, Jean Gallo's son Bill was the best man of Georgette's brother Nicholas. When Bill and brother Frank converted their one-family to a two-family house—a two-year evening/weekend project, done with used nails, studs, and some volunteer labor—Bill lived in the Seminara basement. According to Jean's son Frank: "Mom could work like a construction worker when she had to. I hung plenty of sheet rock with her as my helper." And, from Toni Caggiano, "Jean would have demitasse at night on Mom's [Mary Napolitano's, or Mary Nap's] porch." Into this, Mom/Vina became a "walking delegate:" Georgette's and Mary Nap's houses were always an oasis when Mom did her "Haj" to 86th Street, and I have already mentioned Mom's ministrations to the elderly Seminara sisters on Sunday mornings. But, there is much more.

Jean Gallo was a wiry 5' 2" fireball, diametrically in contrast to the portly Italian Nonna stereotype. To me, mostly from a distance, she was in-your-face, independent, irascible, skeptical and intelligent. But, to Toni and Georgette, who knew her much better, Jean questioned why "bad things happen to good people." It gnawed at her. Bill said his mother was "an iron fist in a velvet glove," but I am also aware, now, that her flinty exterior hid a tender soul. This is more consistent with Mom telling me that Jean listened to her heart, and not her head, when she married dashing and handsome Mr. Gallo. According to Toni, the elder Gallo was "the love of her life. It took her a long time to accept the divorce and his departure when her two boys were ten or eleven."

Jean was a font of love, not only for her two sons and ex-husband, but also for a niece and nephew she raised when their mother succumbed to cancer. So, Bill and Frank had two extra siblings, and Jean was a single mother who raised four teenagers "until they left for college or gainful employment." I do not portray my own upbringing as a modern day Horatio Alger story; I think Jean's boys embody "upward mobility" to a higher degree:

Bill described himself as a typical Bay 26th Street kid. "I decided to take the test for Brooklyn Tech. My [eighth grade] guidance counselor would not authorize me to take the exam; he thought I was a 'wise guy.' Fortunately, my prefect teacher was an Italian lady who used to see me in Church with Mom... a testimony to my good upbringing. [She] went to bat for me. The rest is history. I took to education like I took to street stickball."

I am amazed that Bill had to fight for the right to take the Brooklyn Tech exam. I was in the same junior high school, and felt pushed to take the Stuyvesant exam. So, what did a Brooklyn Tech education get for Bill?

- A full scholarship to Pratt Institute where he finished first in his class, with a Bachelor of Architecture Degree,

- Then, Master of Architecture Degree from Harvard in 1970.

And, Frank is no slouch:

- Graduated State University of New York Maritime College in 1964, second in class,

- Then, first in class in NYU, Stern School of Business Administration in 1971, where he received his MBA.

Momma Jean had something to do with this, duhhh—a single mom, no less. Bill recounts:

> [Mom] passed away at ninety-six after speaking with me on the phone. She was very frail at that point with a failing heart. We were all in Hopetown,

Abaco, Bahamas for my son's wedding. I called to tell her the wedding went wonderfully, and that we all missed her. I know now she hung on for that week just to make sure not to ruin my son's wedding plans. Her last words to me were that she was very cold and tired and that she was so happy for Justin, my son. She said she would get undressed and get into bed to warm up and we hung up. Georgette found her sitting in the same place where we had the phone conversation, peaceful but gone.

Georgette adds, "… at the end of a hard life, she suffered with rheumatoid arthritis that kept her homebound and in constant pain. Nothing relieved it. And, so, Joe—oft-times what you perceived as 'grouchiness' was probably Jeanie enduring pain."

Yes, indeed, a vecchiaia è na carogna.

Jean was the youngest of five children, by ten years. Her father arrived in 1907 with one son, from an area near Loggia, just up the road from Bari. They worked the railroads and in 1913 brought the remainder of the family—Jean's Mom and her other four boys, one of whom died at age thirteen. Jean was the only sibling born in America.

I can ascribe the following to either Bill or Frank: "She was fiercely loyal to our neighborhood and our neighbors. She absolutely adored Nancy & Nick, Rosie & Mary, Vina, Mary Napolitano, Florie & Lily [the Ehrlich sisters], and Tony the Fruit guy."

Tony peddled fruit from his truck, and I asked Georgette if he "had a license." Her response, "We were kids. What did we know about a license?" (I can just picture Florie and Lily saying, "License Schmicense—who *knows* from a license?") Georgette added, "I was only interested in the green pepper he would give me every day for free." So, he had a sweet pepper license. Toni Caggiano reminded me of other itinerant capitalists: The guy who sharpened knives and saws, and the really old fazools, some with horse-drawn carts who picked up cardboard, metal, bottles—recyclers before recycling was cool. One guy had a horse that reminded me of Don

Joseph C. Polacco

Quijote's Rocinante. The horse's name was Giovannina, Giu-annina, or something like that (jew-ah-NEENA). Actually, Don Quijote's horse reminded me of Jewahneena.

I told Bill that his career success was impressive, but that if he were *the* famous Bill Gallo, then I would be really impressed. Even a second cousin, and I would ask for his autograph. So, I had to ask:

"Do you recall Bill Gallo, a cartoonist for the Daily News? He was famous for his caricature of 'dem bums.' When Brooklyn finally won the World Series in '55, The *New York Daily News* had Gallo's work on the cover: a full-faced, crowing bum, almost toothless open mouth yelling 'Who's a Bum *now*?!' Any relation (I mean, to Bill Gallo)?"

Bill responded. "No [no relation], although I own an original cartoon drawing of his depicting Joe DiMaggio which is also signed by Joe himself."

Bill really knows how to hurt a guy. Though I was, and still am, a *Brooklyn* Dodger fan, I would've loved to have that autographed drawing of Joe D, Yankee Clipper by cartoonist Bill Gallo—who I have since learned is of Spanish descent. In any case, Italian subject by Spanish artist of renown would have assuaged some of the pain of this fan, scorned by his Dodgers. I would treasure the Joe D "portrait" as much as an original portrait by the Spanish master Diego Velazquez of Camillo Massimo—almost, but not quite. (Camillo was not a Yankee, but he *was* a Cardinal, predating Dizzy Dean by about three centuries.)

Some of the Bible Study: Rose Seminara, Mom, Nancy (visiting),
Georgette Adams, Mary Seminara, and Jeanie Gallo.
(Missing: Florie Ehrlich and camerawoman Toni Caggiano.)

The Caggianos: Toni, Cara, Vinny, Jennifer,
and Vanessa at Jennifer's Sweet Sixteen party.

Joseph C. Polacco

8. Mom is a Reluctant Star

Vina harbored a timid and humble streak. Of course, she did have a boiling point, just like her sons, and when she was sufficiently "hot," she boiled over to street fighter status—as when she mauled the upstairs lady on the sidewalk. She also had a little bit of show biz in her, which seemed at odds with her humility. (I tend to have a higher show biz/humility ratio, but I *am* a professor.) Mom told me several times about life in her depression-era youth. Her father had long since absconded, with his starlet in tow; grandfather was losing his business and properties. Her mother, my Nonna Nunziatina, found work as a maker of ladies' fine gloves, openly paid less than her male counterparts. She also had to take in two boarders and, at times, cleaned apartments. Older brother Johnny (my late Uncle Jijjie) became a breadwinner and a master carpenter at a very young age—fourteen as I recall. He told me he was the youngest in New York at the time.

In the midst of these tough times, Mom told Nonna Nunziatina that she wanted to stand up in front of an audience and tell stories and jokes. Nonna's response, in dialect of course, went something like: "Pick out a window you want to be thrown out of." They lived on the third floor of a four-story walk-up. So much for a pioneering career in stand-up. I bet that Farfariello could have made good use of Mom. Indeed, Mom maintained a great sense of comedic timing all her life—the "quick quip"—as in when she would puncture Stepdad's posturing. For example, he sported a heavy gold chain with a medallion bearing his initials, "LD," and suggested that Mom get a matching chain, to which she immediately responded—"Yeah, right, I'm going to go around advertising VD."

Brother Michael, however, did graduate from sidewalk Elvis to show biz, both in musical and athletic contexts. In the latter, he twice had occasion to treat Mom to individual limousine service/VIP treatment. But for Mom, VIP meant "Vina Isn't Pompous," or "Vina Is Patient," or "Vina Is Prudent." Vina showed her unassuming side as Michael's guest of honor at the running of the first $100,000 Jordache Los Angeles Pro-Am Marathon. Mom, of course, did not run in the event, but she managed to go from unknown to "Vina IS Popular" after her interactions with the Los Angeles sports and publicity scene. In the April 6, 1981 *Sports Illustrated* article, "Long Run for the Money" by Kenny Moore, Michael had already changed his last name to Grandi, Mom's maiden name.

> But Jordache hadn't really made those [first two pro-am] marathons; it had acted only as sponsor of events organized by others. For the company's third event [1981], the one it looked to as a test case for continued sponsorship, it got lucky. Michael Grandi, [Gayle] Olinekova's boyfriend, had been studying Los Angeles for a couple of years—and feeling embarrassed for it.
>
> "It's such a fine running area, in terms of numbers and quality," he says, "that I was amazed it had no first-class races. Nothing like Boston or New York or Atlanta or 20 other places. I decided that what we could contribute was a great race."
>
> "We" were Grandi, Olinekova and a young boxing and body-building promoter named David Zelon. Together they formed a company called Sun Runners Sports Promotions and bent to such essential details as finding a route to run....

Joseph C. Polacco

When Mom was flown out to Los Angeles for the big day, she felt like a fish out of water. She was at an athletic event, a *celebrity* athletic event, and fearful of leaving our stepdad alone—she almost went back to Brooklyn a couple of times before the big race. Mind you, she prepared meals for him that just needed to be thawed and heated, and his own kids were placed on alert. Michael picked up Mom after her first night in LA, and he found her on her hands and knees scrubbing the bathroom of her hotel suite. "Ma, what are you doin'?!" Her reply was that she did not want the maids to think she was a slob, and after all, "They work so hard."

For the banquet after the big race (won by Ron Fleming and Cindy Dalrymple), a limo picked up Mom. She was decked out in one of her creations (probably cost her $17.34 in 1981 dollars). She *was* an attractive woman going on fifty-six, and her radiant humility did indeed attract attention. When I picture Mom, I think of an owl— perhaps Mom's favorite animal. When friends travelled, they often returned with owl-themed gifts. Mom had those large, radiant, dark eyes, but with a tinge of hazel. One of the guys most captivated by her was the limo chauffeur. Mom insisted on chatting with him, learning about his family, and asking details about his kids. She told Michael and any others who would listen all about this nice young man. And, she was a great hit with the celebrity scene, though in no way seeking to bask in the limelight, nor project her own light, though, of course, she did.

Some time anchor points: In 1981, the year of the pro-am LA marathon, I was in the third year of trying to earn tenure at the University of Missouri-Columbia, embedded in the academic rat-race of research funding, publishing, teaching, committee work, student evaluations, etcetera. Also, as a weekend coach and home-improvement warrior with a young family, I was not nearly as physically or "psychically" close to Mom as I was while living in Hamden, Connecticut (1974-1979). In January 1982, Leonard Sillman had passed, and Michael was living in Puerto Rico and the Virgin Islands, running his own health clubs and running in road races. So Mom's boys were occupied and far from the nest.

However, even at a distance, Mom did indeed inspire feminist Gayle Olenikova, Michael's girlfriend at the time. Gayle featured at least one of Mom's recipes in one of the four books she authored on her own healthy lifestyle and concepts of strength in femininity. I recall Gayle lovingly referring to Vina D'Agostino in her attributions.

Gayle was on the 1972 Canadian national track team, and over her career she ran in events ranging from the 400-meter to the marathon. Gayle combined marathons with competitive body building—a seeming contradiction—and was the subject of an earlier 1981 article in *Sports Illustrated* (January 5) "The Greatest Legs to Ever Stride the Earth," for which Michael provided some of the photography. While both articles featured Gayle as a marathoner, sprinter, and body builder, they also showed that she was multi-dimensional, an intellect and a women's advocate. That she showed real affection for Mom just reinforced my concept of our mother as a champ. It is fitting that both received almost equal billing in the following account by Michael, which he calls the "Brooklyn Cinderella Story."

In spring 1982, my girlfriend and partner, Gayle Olinekova, was announced as the spokesperson for Celanese fibers at a "coming out" at the Waldorf-Astoria. I was so proud and happy that Gayle's achievements were finally being recognized. Gayle was a world-class quarter-miler and marathoner and eventually wrote four books. The third, *The Sensuality of Strength*, (Simon and Schuster), would be released in January 1984.

We very much wanted to share the Celanese announcement with Ma, but she resisted, agreeing only when Gayle insisted she would not be happy unless Ma was at the Waldorf event. Ma was going to take the West End or car service, but we arranged a limousine. Ma was appalled, but agreed when told that Celanese would pick up the tab. (Actually, I did.) Paul Leone, a long-time neighborhood buddy, employed by a large limousine company, couldn't drive Ma. He sent one of his safest and most gregarious drivers who delivered Ma at the Waldorf just as the event was to begin.

Tables were set up for fifty to seventy invited guests, and for the press—magazines such as Vanity Fair, Paris Match, and Der Spiegel, and television reporters and cameramen. On the large stage in front of the room was a huge object draped in red velvet cloth. Gayle, dressed in a simple, rust-colored dress, her blonde hair hanging straight to her shoulders, was just getting up to go backstage to prep. The crowd hadn't yet seen that the large object on stage was a giant photograph of Gayle running, her hair streaming behind her, and the Sports Illustrated caption, 'The Greatest Legs to Ever Stride the Earth.' She was to come out on stage in her formal gown, when the mounted photo would be unveiled. So, as Gayle got up to go backstage, someone said, "Oh, who is that coming through the door? Do we know her?" Heads turned, and the fashionistas looked to see which famous personage had arrived. I looked as well, and then pointed. "Do you mean her?" It was Ma.

I had known my whole life that my mother was beautiful. Of course, every kid loves his beautiful mother, but my friends reinforced my opinion. A petite woman, only about 5'1" or 5'2", Ma still commanded attention in her fifty-seventh year. Her dark eyes flashed when she smiled and her short, wavy, jet-black hair now had threads of silver. She was trim, and wonderfully proportioned, and she was a great model for the clothing she designed and created. And, this night she had really gone all out. Her dress was a silky, form-fitting sheath, black with a red print, and she had made a jacket to go over it, as well as a matching scarf. She was in high heels, with a black hat to match the dress. And she, as a lady did in those days, wore gloves, which I knew she had made herself—she was taught by her own mother. Her jewelry was simple: a gold necklace, a brooch, and her wedding ring. She stood for a moment in the doorway, quietly observing the celebs and wannabees, and then looked directly at me with a blinding smile. I was so stunned I could barely smile back. My mother...Ma... was magnificent.

"What's her name?" asked Patty Munzer, a Celanese representative, and an organizer of the event. "Vina," I said. "Wow! Vina is such a great name for a designer! Do you know her?" "Sure do," I answered. "That's my mother." People around me were commenting on this gorgeous older woman. Even some of the models had stood up to get a closer look. Yep. There she was, in all her well-deserved splendor. My Ma. [Note from bro' Joe: Could you imagine her on the West End subway?]

She sat with us, and a number of the designers and models quizzed her about her dress. Who had designed it? Created it? What company had purchased it? I think she was a bit embarrassed by all the attention, and also, didn't want to admit that she could never afford to buy a dress that spectacular. But she finally gave the answer that floored them: "I made it myself." So, proud son Michael told the enthralled group that both Leonard Sillman and Elinor Gimbel had tried to get her to agree to start a fashion boutique in Manhattan, but she had turned it down. When asked why, I simply said that she had other, more pressing obligations. "Pressing" was as good a word as any, since to Ma it meant standing over an ironing board, carefully pressing our shirts!

Celebration over, and Gayle officially named Celanese spokesperson, we reached Paul's chosen driver. He practically fell all over himself opening the back door, tipping his cap: "There you go, Madam, I even cleaned it for you."

"Oh no, you didn't have to do that," she said looking at the opened back door, and then shook her head. She pointed her finger at him sternly. "Now, you know I'm not going to sit back there all alone. We're friends now." [Bro' Joe's commentary: You can put a Brooklyn girl and a Brooklyn guy in Manhattan, but you can't get the Brooklyn out of them.] He grinned, and slammed the back door shut, opening the passenger door in the front. "Okay Vina, glad to have you up here with me!" I looked on in amazement as my tiny mother climbed into the front seat and smiled at the driver. As he walked around the cab, he smiled at me. "Your mother is a doll! She's an angel!"

Ma rolled down her window so she could kiss me goodbye one more time. "Isn't he just the nicest young man?" she asked. "You know, he's married; oh, and ask him to show the pictures of his daughter at her first communion," she insisted. "His little girl is just beautiful, and so is his wife." The limo driver was already rummaging around in his wallet and digging out photographs of his wife and daughter who were every bit as beautiful as Ma had promised.

The driver smiled at Ma, and told her, "You make yourself comfortable. I'll be ready in a second." He stopped and turned to me, saying, "I couldn't believe it. We were heading toward the Belt Parkway [that runs from Bensonhurst/Bath Beach, along Gravesend Bay, to Queens and Manhattan] when she said, 'Could you pull over, please?'" He shook his head. "I thought maybe she was sick, so I pulled right over, but that wasn't it. She just opened the back door, closed it, then got right into the front passenger seat. She smiled and said, 'It's just not right. I'm sitting all alone in that big back seat, and you're sitting all alone up front. Why can't we just sit together and talk?'"

He shook his head again in amazement. "I couldn't believe it. Boy, your mother is really something special, ya know?" I looked at him and smiled back. "Oh, I know," I said. "Believe me, I know."

When we got home, I called Paul Leone to thank him and to tell him the story of the seating arrangement. Paul interrupted, "I already know. The driver told me all about it. Mike, he even knows her first name, and she knows not only his, but his wife's and daughter's." We laughed. "You know, Michael, we've always said it, but it really is true: Your mother is an angel! She really is."

As Gayle showered, I called Ma, who answered on the first ring. "Oh, hi Mickey!" (As a youngster, and a Mickey Mouse fan, I was affectionately called Mickey.) She continued, "I had such a great time! I was so proud of Gayle and so happy for both of you. And I couldn't believe how many people asked about my dress! I really was amazed! To have that many important people in the fashion industry interested in something I did myself..." She was silent. "It was a special day, wasn't it?" I pawed at a small tear on my cheek. "Yeah, Ma, it really was a very special day...and you're pretty special yourself. I love you." "I love you, too," she replied. "Well, I think all that excitement has pretty well worn me out. I'm going to take a bath and go to bed. Give Gayle my love, and tell her again how proud I am of her...oh, and Mickey...I'm so proud of you, too. Sweet dreams."

And it truly was a special day. Gayle had received the recognition she deserved. And my mother had been admired nearly as much as Gayle because of her talent as a designer and creator of beautiful clothing. I had watched my mother go from a housewife and shop seamstress to an extremely well-dressed, exquisitely beautiful woman in a crowd of women she'd always thought her superiors. I never heard her crow that she was right there at the top

Joseph C. Polacco

with them, but I certainly do, whenever I get the chance to tell the story. My tiny, loving Italian Ma had come through the doorway of a banquet room at the Waldorf-Astoria, and had proven herself to be just as gracious, intelligent, and lovely as any woman in the room. Ma had met the elite of New York City, and she had conquered them. I can never remember a day I was more proud of, or felt more love for, the woman who had raised me. That driver was right—Ma was, and very definitely is, not just a doll…but an angel!

Brother Michael enduring another of his youthful 10-Ks.
Hollywood, California, early 1980s.

Joseph C. Polacco

9. The Binary Vina Star

Mom pronounced her name with a long "I" (VINE-ah). Being proficient in Italian dialects, she knew it was properly pronounced "VEE-na." More than fifty years ago I came across a second Vina (Veena) in Central America, and I will try to trace that journey of discovery from Brooklyn to Cofradía, Honduras. Each Vina had a son, Joe/José, and we have reconnected. Bear with me; the story starts in Bensonhurst.

In 1962 Bensonhurst, many Italian-American male high school graduates rapidly came of age, at least in the sense of financially helping the family. Family could be the one that reared him, or his new family, because there was often an innamorata or fiancée on the horizon, usually within a five-block radius. "Inbreeding depression" was not a problem, because our gene pool was complex, and intermarriage was rampant. Pairings such as Palermitano-Napoletano, Calabrese-Barese, and Abruzzese-Sciacchitano just churned the rich genetic variety of the Mezzogiorno tidal pool. Think of a rich and protean *cioppino* (fish stew). Anything boringly familiar in each spoonful? Inevitably, and increasingly, were admixed even more exotic ingredients: Irish, Greeks, Jews, and other chosen peoples.

For the *giovane*, or youngster, the city provided "good jobs." These included positions with the transit system and the police and fire departments. Other high school graduates learned a "good trade," such as carpentry, plumbing, bricklaying, paving, electrical wiring, welding, and floor covering. Of course, it helped to have family and union connections—often the same thing. The *Baresi* took over the coal and ice businesses. As far as I can tell, neither had a connection to the old country. However, this may explain, in part, our short stocky nature—ice, wrapped in burlap and shoulder-borne, was carried up tenement stairs, and an eighteen-inch block weighed close to 200 pounds. The *Siciliani* dominated asphalt paving—but they came from the land of Mt. Etna and Stromboli. I recall muscled, leathery old fazools in tank tops—"bocce shirts," my brother and I called them—working over a hot tar furnace, in city heat, yelling at each other in dialect. I definitely did not want to mess with these sons of Stromboli. But I would have been taken under Vulcan's wing if I had wanted to enter the trade because, as I explain later, I was an adopted Sicilian. The point here is that a young man could follow his elders, relatives, *compari* or *paisani* (goombahs or countrymen) into a city job or the family business: Doesn't "Polacco & Sons, Ice Dealers" have a nice ring?

But, I had to be different. I wanted to go to college, full-time. And, as a city kid, I wanted to go to arguably the best college in town, Columbia University. I was rejected. I was bitter. I whined. Columbia accepted most of our fencing team—no coincidence that in this arcane sport Stuyvesant was usually the city high school champ, and Columbia a national power. I wanted to play football, and my grades were at least as good as some of the fencers' grades, but no luck. The interview, my first, did not go well. Sheesh, I'm whining now, and I *really* whined then. Mom should have given me a dope slap or a " 'noogie' topside-a my fat head," and just told me to move on. But no, she relayed my plight to the ladies in the dress shop. Her Italian boss overheard and said something to the effect, "I have a friend of a friend (wink), and I think we could pull some strings…" Mom relayed this to Stepdad, and I am thankful he put his foot down, because "Ya never know when the friend will come asking for a favor."

Also, I am sure that Stepdad mentioned to Mom that I could live at home and take the B6 bus to Brooklyn College, a fine city school with minimal tuition, and only thirty minutes from the Bay Parkway–86th Street stop. And, I admitted to falling in love with the "sylvan campus" of Brooklyn College, the site of my Bensonhurst Junior High School graduation. I was not privy to parental financial dealings, at least not then, but in the end I did indeed go to out-of-town Cornell University.

So, one day as I'm returning home from high school during my Senior year, Stepdad greets me in the store: "You got accepted by Cornell." I didn't dwell on his having read my mail, though he was just confirming that the thickness of the envelope indicated an acceptance. So, my only retort was, "Well that's nice—a little late 'cause I'm going to Johns Hopkins." He told me I wasn't, and when I reminded him that we had already sent in a $200 *non-refundable* deposit, he responded with, "No, I called them and they're going to send it back, so you're going to Cornell." I admired his *chutzpah*, a word we dagos didn't use then; it would have been more like, "He had *some* face!" But in retrospect, I'm glad he made that decision for me. And I have to admit that I was very much relieved, even at the time, that the financial burden for all would be a lot less at Cornell.

Why was Cornell a bargain? First, I attended a state-supported division—the College of Agriculture—thereby paying thousands less in tuition than my cohorts in the endowed colleges, such as the College of Arts and Sciences though we walked the same academic halls. For instance, "Artsie" Chemistry majors and "Aggie" Biochemistry majors took the same classes in Mathematics, Physics, Chemistry, etcetera.

Secondly, at Cornell I was able to use my state scholarships. And finally, I worked the summers before and after my freshman year, and *every* paycheck was signed over to Stepdad for deposit into the family "exchequer." I learned later that Stepdad was the conduit for family finances. He was a two-way valve, essentially Chancellor of the Exchequer. Even Mom contributed her seamstress salary, and bought family food and necessities from

Stepdad's weekly allotment. This was probably not unusual in Italian families back in the day.

I am grateful that both parents allowed me to go up to Ithaca. During the Cornell years, Mom sent me fifteen dollars per week for spending money; I seem to recall that Stepdad signed the checks.

But, while I helped finance my education—and this eventually involved a job on campus—I did not work the summer between my sophomore and junior years. I fervently wanted to spend eight weeks of that summer in a Cornell project in rural Honduras. I was selected and I went. So, that summer, instead of contributing to family finances, I further strained them. Mom bore a lot of that strain, though she never complained—not then, not ever. Part of another strain was psychological, and this included being "worried sick" over the whole summer of 1964. There was no Internet, phones were rare, snail mail was incredibly unreliable, and Central America could be dangerous, even then.

However, the Honduras experience was priceless, and it initiated a series of events that traced a path to my currently being married to a Latina. *¡Ayy, caramba!*

And, that summer I met the second Vina in my life. Yes, I am getting to her, as the chapter title might indicate. I was one of ten Cornell students living in the village of Cofradía. We were involved in "community development" in those tumultuous times— three years after the Bay of Pigs, two years after the Cuban Missile Crisis, and eight months after the John F. Kennedy assassination. Those were the early days of the Peace Corps and the Alliance for Progress, and the summer of 1964 also marked the Gulf of Tonkin incident in Vietnam. Our group of students embodied a wide range of political leanings, but we were united in wanting to help improve the lives of the *campesinos*. I think we all knew, implicitly, that our presence would help to win hearts and minds in the face of the Cuban socialist ideal and the Soviet threat. (Cynics might say we were exploited— no better way to put a pretty face on America than through the good deeds of its young people.) Fidel Castro was young and virile, Che Guevara was very much alive and, indeed, guerilla movements were strong in neighboring Guatemala, where Cornell also had at least one student team. As I think back, Mom had just cause for worry, over everything from malaria to a military government. In the midst of all this, we *universitarios* bonded at a very emotional level with our Honduran hosts. Our youthful energy and idealism resonated with the needs and hospitality of the townsfolk.

We were a real treat for Cofradía's young people, so much so that we were always "under the microscope;" observed by a coterie of *cipotes* (young-uns; see-PO-tays). I would advise against using this word today, especially outside of Central America. The cipotes seemed to hang from the rafters and window frames observing us. No matter; I loved the town's kids. I also loved insects, and the tropics. In this "love triangle," I recruited the kids to collect butterflies and exotic beetles for me. One of the unusually earnest and driven cipotes was José, *mi tocayo* (my "namesake"). I would guess he was ten or eleven during that summer when I turned twenty. José would show up in the morning with his buddies, several of them barefoot, to borrow my insect net to collect specimens. He was at our place for demonstrations on mounting them, and for lessons on their natural history. Joselito was indeed intense. I could tell he enjoyed my usual shenanigans, but he listened closely to everything I said about life in the United States, my political opinions and, of course, insect life and nature in general. I could sense him inspecting me as I would go on with some tomfoolery.

Young José took me to his home to meet his mom, and there I learned that she was a Vina. Up until then, I had not known a Vina who was not my mom. And to this day, I have known only two ladies so named. Doña Vina carried herself with grace, and was very at ease in my presence. She was attractive—*trigueña* (olive-skinned), with beautiful expressive and intelligent eyes. Señora Vina de Ayala showed obvious emotion when I told her that my mom was also a Vina. José had two sisters, and I can see, in a picture provided by teammate Patty Patterson, three well-dressed and healthy kids sitting with Mamá Vina on their nicely appointed front porch.

The Ayalas were somewhat better off than most of Cofradía, an unpaved village with its share of illiteracy, poverty, and parasites. We had electricity only in the evening hours, we had to boil our tap water, and we used latrines. The twenty-mile trip to Honduras' second-largest city, San Pedro Sula, was over mostly unpaved roads full of holes and ruts. In 1966, I was team leader in a more distant village, *off* the main road and farther into the countryside, a village with neither running water nor electricity. It seemed to be steeped in melancholy. Cofradía was enlightened, vivacious, and prosperous in comparison.

The important points are that the Bensonhurst–Cornell–Cofradía trail was blazed, and that it is now about to become a round trip facilitated not only by the Vinas, but also by a professional connection. In 2009, I received an email from a certain José Ayala, owner of an animal feed plant in San Pedro Sula. He had seen an article I co-authored, "Quantitative Conversion of Phytate to Inorganic Phosphorus in Soybean Seeds Expressing a Bacterial Phytase." The subject—related to his business—caught his attention, but my name occasioned the email, in which he recited all ten names of our Cornell-in-Honduras team, forty-five years before. José's Vina passed in November 2012, and Joe's Vina in February 2013—a few months apart. We consoled each other on both occasions, and we still communicate—Brooklynese Joe and Hondureño José will always have the Vina bond.

It is amazing how we can overlook specific incidents that are vivid memories to others who shared the same experiences. I was pretty much cut from rough cloth, compared to my nine teammates—all fantastic people, but collectively from a different background. For instance, I was the only one who did not bring a camera—I did not own one. I also brought a single pair of shoes, and I essentially walked out of them—we did a lot of manual work, in addition to literacy training, public health surveys, etcetera. The villagers took pity on "Shoeless Joe," and recruited a local artisan to make me a pair of leather shoes. Man, I was there to help *them*, and they adopted and took care of *me*. Leaving that place was one of the most emotional experiences of my life.

Joseph C. Polacco

I still feel a retro-guilt, because my "rough cloth" was such a contrast to Mom's tasteful clothing and style—well, tasteful to the extent that her economic situation and Singer sewing machine would allow. The Singer was my Nonna's; it had a foot-operated drive, upgraded with an electric motor. So, Joe being underdressed, even for a rural Central American village, had to hurt Mom. And I still feel terrible about my cavalier attitude about my wedding day outfit, five years later. Mom literally begged me to buy new shoes and suit, that very same day.

But Mom, Vina D'Agostino, was instrumental in making my experience in Cofradía a reality. And, Vina de Ayala made it extra special. Don José Ayala has kept that Cornell team in his heart and memory all these years. And now I know why—because Don José's Vina imbued in him a feeling for humankind, just as my Vina did in me:

> Forgive my clumsy translations, Don José: DOÑA VINA DE AYALA WAS ALWAYS VERY GROUNDED IN THE SERVICE OF HELPING OUR COUNTRY-MEN, AND THIS IS THE WAY SHE RAISED US.

Don José wrote the foregoing in upper case; he then went on, with incredible detail, about his experiences of service and growth, and how important we Cornell students (and the "Pueblo de los Estados Unidos") were to those efforts.

> We, together with the Cornell students and Peace Corps members, including Mr. Holger Jorgensen, made blocks of *barro* [adobe] and cement for construction of the walls of the elementary school and *Centro de Salud* [clinic] for *all* of the inhabitants of the town.

Holger Jorgensen was a Danish-born naturalized American who became a Peace Corps agronomist at a fairly advanced age—advanced, at least, from my youthful perspective.

In the evening, everyone participated in the 'Concert of the Cornellians.' They were led by Guillermina (Billie), a pretty *gringuita* who played the guitar, and other students played the sax, the clarinet, etcetera.

Billie was also our team leader, and had to put up with José Polacco—she would have been a great baseball manager. She was a gifted *guitarrista*, and it seemed that *all* Hondurans were born with an innate ability to play the instrument. And, the guys loved doing duets with Billie. While on the musical theme, I *must* mention that I was imprinted with the Cumbia that summer—a Colombian folk dance popularized now from Mexico to Perú, and not unknown to Columbia, Missouri.

On some afternoons, we played sports, and got to know the ball for American football that looked like a pumpkin seed, something we had never seen.

Tutico [Stu] was another young American who lived in Milparado, another very poor village. He would sometimes visit fellow Cornell students 'camped' in Cofradía. [And, a little gossip; we all knew he was sweet on Billie.]

It was an unforgettable experience, and it instilled in my life the desire to be successful, *un triunfador* [a winner]. Almost all of us cried the day we went to the airport to say goodbye.

And we did too, José, as you know. We sobbed shamelessly.

They had won our hearts, and those memories have never been forgotten. I looked for those students, until fifty years later I found them, and now I share social media communication with some of them at least. I hope to see them in person real soon.

Me too, Don José.

After some prodding, I got Don José to trace his successful career from his beginnings in Cofradía. It is indeed impressive, and that look of intensity on his young face was a true indicator of a driven young man. *But*, and I keep coming back to this, his dad, and his mom, Vina, helped to channel that ambition and drive to help his fellow man:

So, Vina de Ayala was always there for people less favored, and in this she helped my father in his commercial and social activities. José R. Ayala, Senior, was the treasurer of the *Comité Pro-Mejoramiento de Cofradía* [Committee for the Advancement of Cofradía], and in my house he sold tickets that allowed patients to receive medical care and medicines in the Health Center. The cost for each ticket was 0.50 Lempira, or USD $0.25. In my house we also kept the milk and cheese donated by the people of the U.S.A., under the Alliance for Progress program; these dairy products were for the town's children. There were other activities, such as teaching the *amas de la casa* [female family heads] to make fruit preserves, pickled vegetables, and cured meats. This latter program was sponsored by STICA (*SERVICIO TÉCNICO INTERAMERICANO DE COOPERACIÓN AGRÍCOLA*) [Inter-American Technical Service of Agricultural Cooperation], another U.S.A. program. From these activities was born my great feeling for two things: agriculture and the people and government of the United States.

My mother always helped her peers without ever seeing any innate difference, of any kind, among them, no matter their need. She was not political, but very humane and supportive.

I have composed this VINA ACROSTIC:

Vuestra nobleza siempre disponible
Inmediata para quien la necesite
Nunca indiferente a los demás
Alma buena la de nuestras Mamás.

"No sabía de mi talento literario! [You didn't know of my literary talent!]"

José, 'mano (bro'), once in a while I write a Valentine's poem, in Spanish, even. This is a poor rendition of my own Vina Acrostic:

Virtud simple, de alma poderosa
Indómita, con pasión tan generosa
Ninguna motivación egoista, sino
Amor pa' ambos: el rico y el campesino.

Yes, I know, my version needs work. Let me further embarrass myself by trying to put our Acrostics into English rhyme, without too much mangling of meter and meanings:

José's Vina:
Valued, your nobility, always at the ready
Immediate help for the needy and unsteady
Never indifferent to the world around
A motherly soul; your goodness abounds

Joe's Vina:
Virtues, simple but from a powerful soul
Indomitable, with generous passion unfold
Never a selfish motive, even self-abnegation
A love for all, no matter their life station.

You're an inspiration, Don José, and our collaborating on this story, fifty-plus years after our encounter, is not completing a cycle, but reinforcing our mutual orbit around the Binary Vina Star.

Joseph C. Polacco

Doña Vina with children,
Delmis, José (Josélito), and
Lourdes.

Joselito, center, with entomologist
colleagues.

Photos courtesy Patty Patterson

José, el mayor (José, the elder), demonstrating the fine art of
mounting butterflies. I have no idea about the puppet being
spied by Joselito off my left shoulder. Photos summer 1964,
Cofradía.

10. Letter from the Kiwanians

Stepdad was active in the local Democratic Club, and member in good standing in an 86th Street merchants' organization. He also had an affinity with the NYFD and NYPD unions—his son and son-in-law were, respectively, a firefighter and a detective. He left issues of the Policemen's Benevolent Association magazine showing through his car's rear window—he was not too shy to show connections especially if he was illegally parked. I remember vividly the more congenial community connections that he and Mom had as members of the local Loyal Order of Moose Lodge, on 18th Avenue and 77th Street.

The Moose were a philanthropic and community-minded organization, but I mostly recall their great parties—virtuosos of the cha-cha-cha almost intimidated me from getting on the floor, but not *quite*. Their collective humor was, well, gavoonish. ("Mr. Bacciagaluppo, in our sex survey, you, a man of ninety-two years, say that you have sex every night of the week, fifty weeks of the year? *Thassa right*. So, what about the other two weeks? *Well, thassa when-a the guy who picksa me up and takesa me down has the vacation. Ba da boom.*") I have several banquet photos of four or five ladies seated at a table, with their husbands standing behind, each with two hands on his spouse's shoulders. How would Margaret Mead have interpreted this? Call me biased, but Mom was always the cutest, trimmest, and best-dressed of the ladies. *And* she could dance.

Vina and Lou were buddies with the parents of long-time actor Tony Lo Bianco (*The French Connection* [William Friedkin, Director, 1971] and twenty-five other movies). I believe both couples were part of the 18th Avenue Moose and that they interacted socially inside and outside of the club. Mom told Michael that the Lo Biancos were "very nice people."

The Moose Lodge is still there on 18th Avenue, but Vina and Lou changed over from the Moose to the Kiwanis. Indeed, Stepdad became active enough to be elected to a one-year term as president of the local (Mapleton) Kiwanis chapter. I suspect that Marty and Maureen Neuringer had a lot to do with my parents' move, and also with their both being active participants. Of course, Mom did not need much prodding to get very involved in Kiwanis charitable and fund-raising activities. She was loved and she loved participating. After Stepdad passed, Mom and I, sometimes accompanied by Nancy, used to walk to their meetings—Mom being a great walker, and these were prodigious walks—but Marty and Maureen Neuringer often gave her a lift.

So, who are Marty and Maureen Neuringer, and how are they related to Vina? I was prodded to recall Marty's "Kiwanism" when I found a coffee mug in my Columbia, Missouri home, engraved: "Brooklyn Kiwanis, Martin Neuringer, Lieutenant Governor 1993-1994." But, Marty, Maureen, Lou and Vina have deeper roots. Marty and his dad were floor-covering competitors of my stepfather. And Marty's brother Allen is a beloved Emeritus Professor of Psychology at Reed College in Portland, Oregon, where my son Benjamin spent four years—five, counting the year he waited for his fiancée to finish. While on the subject of Reed, I have to say that Mom was one of the better dancers at their graduation gala, and she passed those dance genes through me to my sons, Benjamin and Joseph. But, I don't want to brag about my kids because Mom taught me that bragging invites the malocchio.

Marty and Maureen evoke Brooklynite Mel Brooks and Bronx-born Anne Bancroft (*née* Anna Maria Italiano), Mel's wife of forty-one years until she passed in 2005. Marty and Maureen are a funny and dynamic Jewish-Italian (Neapolitan even, *oy vey!*) pair, as were Mel Brooks and Anne Bancroft, who was Siciliana. Marty has great material: he just needs a better agent. I could just see him say that "Kiwanis" is the fifth Hebrew letter on the *dreidel*. Mom had the qualities that attracted people of character like Marty and Maureen. And Mom knew the dreidel song. ("*Dreidel, dreidel, dreidel, I made it out of clay…*")

One night Marty treated his Kiwanis club—mostly Italian, mind you—to a Passover Seder, edifying, if not filling, until of course, when Elijah the prophet did not show, non-kosher food was served by meeting host La Bella Panini (13th Avenue and 70th Street). Marty's dad, so different from many of his kin, had a vacation/retirement home in New Hampshire, and *not* Florida; oy gefilte. Then again, there are definite similarities to the New England moves made by Bernie Sanders and the ice cream entrepreneurs, Ben Cohen and Jerry Greenfield—three fine examples of the Brooklyn tribe who found their promised land in Vermont after the Brooklyn exodus. Returning from New Hampshire one day, Marty, a man after my own heart, found a turtle on the shoulder of a Vermont highway—a near road-kill. Marty nursed him back to health, and three-legged "Montie" lived many years, and was a favorite of Brooklyn school children. I was thinking that Marty, Maureen, and Montie also had a python, but that Monty Python thing was probably an invention of wishful thinking. And, Maureen confirmed that it was a boa constrictor (dang it).

So, I am connected to the Neuringers in floor covering, love of reptiles, Reed College, and the Kiwanis. And Mom is the common factor. Maureen, bless her heart, has written about Mom:

> Here is a remembrance of your remarkable Mom. My husband joined Kiwanis in 1987. Marty was part of the 86th Street Bath Beach Kiwanis Club, where we first met your mom. Quickly, Vina and I hit it off, and we talked about our connections—my family was Neapolitan, and I was married to a Jewish man (*meshugganah*, just crazy,

pazzo). We all grew up in Bensonhurst. We talked about how similar Italian and Jewish mothers were, and that their major theme was eat, eat, and *eat*. We shared the Seinfeld joke, "I teach him shame and he teaches me guilt." We both laughed and laughed about that. [Jerry Seinfeld is also from the 'hood.]

I remember Vina's warm friendliness. On one occasion, the club asked for donations from its members, which were to be sold in a benefit raffle. My husband Marty, like Louie D'Agostino, was in the floor-covering business, and we decided to donate an area rug. On the day of the event, I helped Marty roll and tie the rug to the top of our car. No sooner did we step outside than it started to pour. We wrapped the rug in plastic, and off we went, and the rain did not stop. At La Bella Panini, we untied the rug. I placed the back on my left shoulder, and Marty took the front on his left shoulder. We walked through the long restaurant—past the kitchen and into the back meeting room—area rug on our shoulders. We were greeted by Vina, who offered a dry towel, and we settled into our seats with a nice glass of wine. To support the club, we purchased raffle tickets from Vina. And, *we won!*—we won the area rug *we* brought to the restaurant. Your mom and I laughed so hard we almost wet our pants. When the meeting was over, the rug went back on our shoulders, through the long restaurant, and onto the top of Marty's car. Vina said, "No good deed goes unpunished." And it didn't.

Vina was a born volunteer. She gained much pleasure in helping others. We all settled in the Mapleton Kiwanis Club. One of our many projects is feeding families at the Manhattan Ronald McDonald House. The families are sheltered at the house free of charge and have seriously ill children going through treatment at New York hospitals. They are transported to doctor meetings and treatments as needed. In the evenings, the Kiwanians donate time to bring and serve meals to sick children, siblings, and parents. In the summertime, we sponsor a barbecue with all the fixings. President Joe Corace mentioned, almost in passing, "We need aprons with Kiwanis names on them." Within the week, Vina gifted us with over a dozen aprons, sewn to perfection. No fuss, no muss; Vina used her talents to help others yet again. The next barbecue, everyone wanted one of her aprons. We still proudly wear them today in her honor.

Vina took the club to the Holy Family Home to host a Valentine's Day party for the residents. We provided food, treats, and most of all, *music*. Following her lead, we danced—even with people in wheelchairs—and we couldn't help but smile all the time, knowing we made a difference in the lives of these people. The happy residents wanted to know, 'When are you coming back?' I even heard someone tell Vina, 'I need a button sewn on my sweater.' She was way younger than Vina. When your mom came on the next Tuesday, of course, she promptly sewed the button on. Vina never received a dime for all her sewing, and doll-making, which she did well into the time her treatments began.

"Read Around the World" was another project Vina wholeheartedly supported. The club purchased soft-covered books, and went off to local schools to give them away. Each child received two books of his/her choice. Vina helped the children sign their names in the books so they could feel the pride of ownership. Vina was great with the children. She sat in a small group and read a book with great expression. You could see the excitement in the children's eyes as they listened to her stories. We did this many times, and Vina was always the first to volunteer. I could see her love of education being shared with these children.

Joseph C. Polacco

The last and probably most touching story is about the holiday parties for battered women's children in a local shelter. Vina helped wrap almost forty age-appropriate toys for children each year, for over fifteen years. These children left their homes for safety with nothing but the clothes on their backs—usually in the middle of the night. They would have had nothing for the holidays if not for us. Vina gave out drinks, cookies, and candy. She bowled with the makeshift bowling game we rigged up so kids could win prizes. She danced to "Feliz Navidad," making a circle with the children, who were filled with joy. She helped lift children onto Santa's knee to receive their gift. We all saw that we got much more than we gave.

To Maureen's accolades, I have to add my own to Marty, Maureen and the rest of the Kiwanians. During Mom's chemo regime, I accompanied her, Maureen, Sandy, and other fantastic ladies to a night at a Ronald MacDonald House in Manhattan. Marty was already there, and he was de *man*. To the kids and their parents he was avuncular. To me, he was a drill sergeant; I had to divvy up the food, properly and with forethought, to make sure all were served. Mom? Well, Mom also was both good cop and bad cop. Her heart broke for the kids, but she was also the custodian of the food—it was for the kids and their parents; no moochers. And the great leadership of our Kiwanis, at the neighborhood and New York State level, is carried on by Joe Corace. Joe told me "Your mother was very much loved."

Photos courtesy Marty and Maureen Neuringer

Marty and Maureen Neuringer. 1992. Note the traditional "hands on woman's shoulders" pose.

Joe, Mom, and Marty after a local Kiwanis chapter meeting.

Joseph C. Polacco

The serving crew after a stint at the Ronald McDonald House.
Left to right: Joe, Eileen LaRuffa, High-kicking Mom, Nancy,
Sandy Irrera, and two mystery ladies.

Reading Assistance at a local public school.

11. D'Agostino Clan. The Teachers

The teachers are related to my stepdad, Ludovico D'Agostino. The kinship seemed natural: The teachers are learned, and Ludovico (Lou) was mainly self-taught. He became known as "Doc" because of his interest in/knowledge of medicine and his aptitude for tinkering in electronics, autos, etcetera. Before I get to the teachers, I want to establish the D'Agostino family, of which they are a part. Stepdad came into Mom's life when I was about five. They both brought "baggage" into their oft-unhappy relationship. However, Lou did come to bat for me, and for Mom, on many occasions. I never looked for, nor resented, signs of favoritism for his biological over his "inherited" kids. He did indeed show real pride in my academic and familial accomplishments, and he truly loved my own three kids. And, I called him Daddy, not Stepdad. He was Grandpa to my kids. Though he was of the "old school," he admired my feisty, German-American wife, and seemed to support her gender-based battles against the academic establishment. He loved a winner, no matter the weight class.

However, to me, the best aspect of Lou D'Agostino was his large extended family, which included the teachers. Stepdad was our entry, and Mom cultivated the rich soil of the D'Agostino clan: They became my *cugini* (cousins), paisani, my "goombahs." I always felt like part of *la famiglia*. This mixed-breed Barese-Napoletano felt like a real Siciliano in their company.

Joseph C. Polacco

This was important to me, but especially to Mom, because her own close relatives and siblings had emigrated to Los Angeles, Las Vegas, Chicago, and other far-away places, and most passed well before she did. Indeed, kid sister Angelina died suddenly at 26 years, not long after moving to Vegas—a huge blow to Mom, and an event that almost resulted in our adopting my cousin "Little" Ben. It did not happen—three boys sharing a bed in back of our store was too much, though Aunt Vina would have made it work. And Michael and I thought it fun the few times the arrangement was tried out. "Little Ben" was eventually adopted by his Uncle Ben, in LA, but he still has a special place in his heart for his Aunt Vina.

The important point was that in Brooklyn, if you could not walk to visit relatives, they were ipso facto "far away." So, separation hurt Mom, to the extent that she often mentioned it, though she had learned over the years to internalize most of her pain. La famiglia D'Agostino helped fill that empty space in Mom's heart.

La famiglia had its origin in Belmonte Mezzagno, a *paese* (village) just south of Palermo. Wikipedia informs us that in local dialect it's Beddumunti Minzagnu, and the second name seems more familiar to me. The website also informs that this village is "famous for its olive oil and goat's milk cheese," and is the birthplace of Benedetto Spera, Mafioso convicted *in absentia* for the killings of anti-mafia judges Paolo Borsellino and Giovanni Falcone. I might add that Mom learned the dialect, though it was almost useless when trying to communicate with folks from other paesi, even within Sicily.

John D'Agostino, Ludovico's dad, married *una signorina* also by the D'Agostino surname, and with the first name "Jackie" (Gioacchina? Giacomina?). Though they shared a last name in a village of about 5,000 inhabitants at the turn of the twentieth century, they maintained that they shared no blood. And indeed, their four sons were all healthy and competent. The effect was to link two large families, and I am always coming across D'Agostinos, from Columbia, Missouri to Hamden, Connecticut. A D'Agostino family reunion in Vineland, New Jersey in the late '70s had participants from Texas to Sicily, and these geographical extremes seemed to be reflected in height, bearing, and certainly in dress. And, that reunion was so typical of the family: In our Sunday best, we played a softball game on concrete, with sliding and all. Later that day, two D'Agostino *belle donne* (beautiful ladies) got into a "donne-brook." Ahhh, it's great to be Sicilian—it's like high-test Italian. And I love that *Belladonna* is both a poisonous and a beautiful plant. *Prima donna*? Well, you don't have to be Italian—or a lady—to be one.

In New York, at least in Manhattan, everyone knows of "D'Agostino— New York's Original Grocer." I count thirteen Manhattan locations, in Greenwich Village, Hell's Kitchen, Kips Bay, Morningside Heights, Murray Hill, Sutton Place, Upper and Lower East Side, and even an outlier in Westchester County. I was always impressed with their appropriation of the "Dag Bag," undaunted by the similarity to dago. And, just think of the possibilities— a line of semolina-enriched bagels: "Dagbag-els." Of course, if I were a manager in charge of publicity, the chain would have gone out of business long ago. I don't think they share too much consanguinity with the D'Agostinos I grew up with. But, who knows? All Italians are cousins.

But, I digress. Ludovico had a first cousin, also a Lou D'Agostino, who ran a real estate business in the Gravesend neighborhood of Brooklyn. His office was next to a *salumeria & latticini freschi* (sausage and fresh dairy [cheese] store), an Italian deli. The initial walk upstairs to his apartment was always an overwhelming olfactory experience— ahhh, they don't make provolone like that anymore. New York is not just bustle, noise, and multi-colors, but also a kaleidoscope of aromas.

Uncle Lou and Aunt Fannie eventually moved to a lovely home on Ocean Parkway that, in the very old days, was a promenade to the then-fashionable Coney Island. Their younger daughter's family took over the apartment, and the building, which was on very busy Avenue U, next to another El line (the F, which runs along MacDonald Avenue). However, the backyard was in a different world, and was much larger than Mr. Spadaro's Sicilian paese enclave, and probably larger than most Sicilian subsistence farms. Lou's dad (Uncle Pete) raised chickens, and cultivated fruit trees, and all manner of vegetables, strawberries, basilicó, etcetera.

He and his old fazool buddies used to play pinochle in a tree house, which I am sure he built with his own hands. I recall one summer night, as we were chatting around the kitchen table, Lou's dad would come in every forty-five minutes or so to load up on more beer, wine, and treats to take to his buddies, a cigarette hanging from his lower lip (or was it a de Nobili stogie? We called them "guinea stinkers").

Uncle Lou was successful and conservative, a disciplinarian and a man of respect (in the best possible sense of that phrase), and he seemed to know a lot more than how to buy and sell properties. His opinions were always well thought out and well expressed. I loved him because he was very into education and thinking outside of the box. He loved that I loved insects and spiders, and that I had interests in science in general. He engaged me in serious conversation about my interests and ambitions. One of the best moments of my youth was when he told his cousin, my stepdad, "He's (Joseph is) O.K."

Yes, dear reader, I am getting to the teachers. Lou and Fannie raised two upstanding young ladies. Rosalie, the elder, graduated from St. John's University to a teaching career in New York parochial and public schools. Rosalie married another Sicilian-American, James (Jim) Mangano. They met at St. John's. Jim and Rosalie are joined at the hip. In fact, they sign their communications with a hybrid name, which I will signal here as "JR." JR were Mom's beloved "teachers," and indeed Jim spent many years at Sheepshead Bay High School, where he was an award-winning English teacher. I learned of his award from the newspaper, and congratulated him, and he never mentioned it again. To Mom, the teachers—her name for them— were a source of joy, comfort, and support in her life.

JR are equally at home with pasta fazool, dim sum, filet mignon, Greek lamb from a spit, or *sfinciunnu* (a non-intuitive, but delicious blend of onions and breadcrumbs which can be a topping on focaccia or Sicilian pizza). JR introduced Mom and me to the works of Isamu Noguchi, famous Japanese-American sculptor and landscape designer. We were touring his exhibit somewhere in the wilds of Astoria, Queens, when JR started to engage in multiple bows with a Japanese visitor. Of course, having done a two-year sabbatical in Japan, they spoke fluent Japanese (in addition to the argot of Beddumunti Minzagnu). Turns out the lady at the museum knew Isamu as a lad.

JR are consummate fishermen. Note that Sheepshead Bay was where you went in Brooklyn to go on a fishing boat. And, Sheepshead Bay High School tried to dissuade Jim from retiring because, as they said, "You are a fantastic teacher," to which he replied, "Yes, but I'm a *much* better fisherman." JR travel the world fishing fresh and salt waters, be they streams, rivers, lakes, lagunas, bays, or beachfronts. Their interactions with locals must be hilarious—who ever heard of such consummate trout fishermen with such a deep Brooklyn brogue? The teachers always regaled Mom with a *pesce* usually caught in the local waters, such as Long Island surf or the "bite" around New York City. She so loved preparing the fish with them *nella cucina*. Their cooking was a polyglot medley of food prep, gossip, laughter, and operatic interludes. JR really were Mom's guardian angels—among others, of course—and never accepted thanks for "being there" because, as they put it, "She is a blessing in our lives." Their retirement lifestyle combines six warm months in lower Manhattan, with six months in their Florida home.

Just before we learned of Mom's cancer recurrence in Fall 2011, Nancy and I visited New York on the way back from a trip to Uruguay. After visiting a Soho sculpture exhibit of Cecilia Míguez (Nancy's best friend from Uruguay—a sculptress firmly established in Los Angeles for at least thirty years), we dined, not at a Soho five-star, but at a neighborhood family Dominican restaurant, El Castillo de Jagua II on Grand Street: Rosalie, Jim, Jim's bro' John, Nancy, Mom, and I. The staff knew JR, who were regulars. A waitress brought over pictures of her new nephew, and Rosalie and Mom oohed/ahhed over the *niñito*. And, *of course*, Jim made great recommendations from the menu. Just a short reminiscence over the years recalls our dining in Turkish, Chinese (in Chinatown, of course), Italian, Spanish, Indian (in Jackson Heights, Queens), and Harlem soul-food restaurants and, more recently, in a fantastic Sicilian seafood place: Rocco's Calamari on Tenth Avenue in Brooklyn.

Joseph C. Polacco

In 2005, I was on sabbatical in Mar del Plata, Argentina. During our sojourn, I was invited to the remote town of La Rioja, where I gave some talks, a radio interview, and a class on bio-ethics, of all things. Nancy accompanied me, and while in the region, we went to the wilds of the Andean foothills, visiting a national park full of geological formations and *algarrobo* trees: source of the famous carob. If parched La Rioja is remote, the twin Provincial Park, Talampayo/Ischigualasto (Valle de la Luna in San Juan Province) in the "rain shadow" of the Andes, is almost lunar. Unbeknownst to us, back in Bensonhurst, Mom fell while visiting Marie D'Agostino, and broke her pelvis. She was immobile, and the hospital wanted to release her, days before she was ready to fend for herself, and while I was still ignorant of the occurrence. Mom, though a tough, independent lady, knew she was not ready to leave. JR interceded. They can be *very* persuasive, and Mom stayed an extra three days, complete with physical therapy. JR wanted no thanks or acknowledgment—they were just doing "the bizzhi-*ness*," as Mario Puzo might have said. They delayed a trip to Florida to intercede on Mom's behalf.

Another lesson in not getting too far from Mom: I learned of the first detection of a breast lump, in 2004, while in the mountains outside of Madrid. News reached me from my ex-wife, Mary Schaeffer, by way of her email to a Spanish colleague who called my Spanish host's landline to tell me, "*Tu madre está mal.*" (Your mother is sick.) I was at least able to accompany Mom to the lumpectomy, again at Maimonides, some weeks later.

So, the teachers provided joy, company, great food, moral and practical support for mom. She loved them dearly. How could I ever repay, or reciprocate? How about a feeble linguistic/cultural interlude—the following open letter:

Dear Teachers,

I am eternally grateful for the love and care and attention you provided Mom. As English teachers having diverse fluency that ranges from Sicilian dialects to Japanese, you may appreciate some of our linguistic experiences in Argentina. Some occurred while you were dealing with Mom— the broken pelvis, the hospital stay, and all the rest of the camurria. (Back to you, dear reader: *camurria* is annoyance that never goes away, like the linguistically related gonorrhea.)

As you may know, Nancy and I were in ex-president Carlos Menem's province (La Rioja). Menem is a palindrome, and it seems that Argentina is replete with palindromes. For example, Neuquén is a province. Palindromic Menem, once considered a savior, fell from grace for purported corruption, before running for president <u>again</u> (that back and forward trait). His very junior ex-wife was Cecilia Bolocco—actress, designer, model and former Miss Chile and Miss Universe. There is a play-on-words joke about their marital relationship, but it's in Spanish and probably not too repeatable in any language. Language, however, is only a partial barrier to appreciating the incredible palindromes of the mystical Argentine genius, Juan Filloy, who published at least 8,000. Filloy was also a judge for thirty years, founded a soccer team, and arranged fights for Luis "Wild Bull of the Pampas" Firpo. I cannot resist mentioning that his books, published after his thirty-year hiatus on the bench, all had seven-letter titles (Ignitus, Yo, yo y yo, Gentuza, Vil & Vil, Tal Cual, La Purga, Elegías, *and* Sexamor) *except for* Los Ochoa, *which had eight* (ocho, *naturally*).

But, there are more language, literature, and even sports connections between Bensonhurst and Argentina. Fifty years before I went to Argentina, Stepdad and I were "bonding" over boxing—prizefighting, which I now know to be an abomination, something Mom always knew. So, I knew about Juan Filloy's boy, Luis Firpo, and I knew that he lost to Jack Dempsey in New York's Polo Grounds (in 1923, when its New York Giants owners ruled New York baseball). But, the circumstances were murky, and indeed, Dempsey may have survived a KO by the creative ineptitude of a ref. Some Argentines claimed they knew the "real" story—Argentines, like we Americanos, have a sense of exceptionalism. So, I looked at the old footage. Dempsey knocked Firpo down seven times, the last one a winning KO in the second round. If the fight were held today, Dempsey would have been declared the winner after the third first-round knockdown of

Joseph C. Polacco

the Wild Bull. However, Firpo also knocked Dempsey out of the ring in the first, and Dempsey may have been helped back in by ringside reporters—clearly a disqualification. A light signaling a Firpo victory was momentarily lit on Buenos Aires' famed Palacio Barolo, opened earlier in 1923. Teachers, you would love, and probably already know, that this building's 100 meters, twenty-two floors of reinforced concrete, represent the 100 cantos of The Divine Comedy. *There are many links between Argentina and Italy, but exploring them is not my purpose here. Next time we get together over sfinciunnu, and of course a glass of Barolo, we will pontificate/chiacchierare.*

—Con molto affetto, Joe.

While fact-checking, I received the following from JR:

> "...as to the memoir, it was accurate and poignant. You were very sweet to say the kind things you said about us. Thank you. But the true hero(ine), as always, was Vina. Your words sometimes evinced a tear. Not because they were maudlin or overly sentimental, but because they portrayed her and our relationship so well. Once again we were reminded of how much we miss her and how large a void her passing left in our lives. We're so glad you undertook this project. Love to you both. JR

Jim Mangano with a polpo/octopus
that will become a fantastic dish.

Joseph C. Polacco

Rosalie, not to be outdone, with a pesce
that she undoubtedly caught off a Florida beach.

Photos courtesy Jim and Rosalie Mangano

Lunch at El Castillo de Jagua II.
Left to right: John Mangano, Rosalie, Vina, Jim, Joe, Nancy.

12. D'Agostino Clan. Uncle Gregory

Stepdad had three brothers: Frank, John, and Gregory, in that order. The Sicilian custom was to name the first-born son after the father's father, hence Frank. Frank became a prodigal son who left New York, changed his last name to something like "Buxley," and lived more of the American dream—which to me was Kraft casseroles and never-ending episodes of *Leave it to Beaver*. John ran a car repair place out of his home a few large blocks down 86th Street, towards Coney Island. He was entertaining, and seemed to love—and to encourage—the insanity of his kids and grandkids, who appeared to live almost permanently with him and his wife Catherine.

But—Uncle Gregory—*he* was my hero. He, his immediate family, and I were probably the only Brooklyn Dodger fans in the D'Agostino clan. He was a shield against my front-runner Yankees fans cousins, and even my brother. The Yanks won five straight World Series from 1949 to 1953, and eight out of twelve from 1947 to 1958, the first year of the LA Dodgers franchise. They made a habit of beating the Dodgers in the Series: '41, '47, '49, '52, and '53. Sure, dem bums beat the Yanks in '55, but the Yanks returned the favor in '56 (Don Larson? *A perfect game?* Wha?! A sure sign of the apocalypse.) Destiny was not with us, and the apocalyptical end times started in '58, when the LA Dodgers were playing in front of beach boys and Hollywood idols.

Joseph C. Polacco

Uncle Gregory was always there, literally, because he was Stepdad's installation guy. The store was even named after him: Greg's Floor Covering, so when he was in the store he was actually in our home. My stepdad knew enough Yiddish to "pass," and some of his patrons even called him "Meestah Ghrrregh." Oh, did I mention that Uncle Gregory, and his wife Millie and kids, became dyed-in-the-wool Mets fans in '62? As Jimmy Breslin said of *all* Mets fans, "They were Mets fans all their lives." (Stepdad was not into baseball, but we did connect, for example, over the Monday night program, *Boxing from St. Nicholas Arena.*)

So, Uncle Gregory was in my home when he worked. And I never really could separate work from home. For instance, leaving for a date or other important encounter such as stickball or pick-up basketball, I had to go through the store or else climb over two back fences and violate neighbors' airspace. Stepdad could intercept and ask me to help Uncle Greg on a job. "Helping" meant moving furniture, heaving rolls of floor covering up four-story walk-ups, and otherwise keeping Uncle Greg company. The company was good; he was so funny, often feigning attacking a kvetch of a customer with his carpet knife. Especially with Jewish customers, he would tell them, "He's going to college." When they oohed and aahed, he would add: "He's taking up time and space." And tips, man, he was generous with them—I always got a major cut, if not all of it.

I can almost put a date on it, the "it" commemorating how "family always comes in handy." School was over after my sophomore or junior year in college. I was watching the Mets blow another one, this time to the Reds. The Reds' centerfielder, Vada Pinson, stumbles but still makes a game-ending catch with runners in scoring position in brand-new Shea Stadium. I'm guessing a Saturday (May 15, 1965?). Why is this important? Well, at the same time as the catch, a battle royal breaks out at 2238 86th Street in Greg's Floor Covering. Uncle Gregory's family, and a few others, are in the backyard. (Since I was now in college, the garden plot was in disuse, and eventually, ugh, was paved over.) Mom is cooking in the kitchen, my bro' catching Vada Pinson's catch on the tube.

Before I get to Stepdad, let me say this about him: I never saw him back down from a fight, in or out of the store. Twice, on the road, I saw crazy, angry young guys threaten to break his nose. This was road rage before it had a name. Stepdad's schnozz was already especially aquiline for having been broken a couple of times—an environmentally enhanced trait, or, as geneticists would say, a maximized G X E (gene by environment) interaction. When confronted both times with an offer of yet another free "nose job," he just sez: "Oh yeah? Let's see you try." And both times, he was in the driver's seat of his car, with the window down, and his nose such a tempting target. One guy was a motorcycle honcho, with his gang in tow, and the other a pazzo trying to pass us on a one-way single-lane street as Stepdad looked for an address to deliver a roll of linoleum. I don't think my own presence in the passenger seat was much of a deterrent. Oh, and both times the guys just walked away cursing.

Okay, back to the store: two guys walk in on Vada Pinson Saturday and confront Stepdad. They were *gingerillas*, as my Uncle Greg would say, and I have no idea what that means—but picture two beefy guys with muscle shirts and tattoos, before tattoos were cool. The older guy sez, "You said you were going to trim my linoleum, and you never came around, and my daughter-in-law is pregnant and fell over the 'buckle.'" (In those days, un-cemented linoleum had to "stretch," necessitating a follow-up visit to trim the edges and seams—also a second chance to make up for installation mistakes.) "If she loses the baby, I'll kill you." Stepdad says something like, "Let me see you try." The older guy hauls off and punches, just as Uncle Greg walks in. Fists were flying, and some very heavy vertical rolls of linoleum were falling in chain reaction. (Who ever heard of bracing rolls to the wall in those days? OSHA? Fahgeddaboudit.) Uncle Greg is taking on the young guy, linoleum timbers falling over his back, and grabs an aluminum pipe, and repeatedly hits him over the head as the guy is bull-rushing him—each kink in the pipe a testimony to battle. Stepdad's nose is broken yet again. The ladies in the back are screaming. Bro' tries to join the fray, but he later

Joseph C. Polacco

claimed that when he tried to enter the melee, he was always kicked back, as if by a gale-force wind. The cops show up, and so does an ambulance.

The older guy winds up in Coney Island Hospital, and la famiglia is notified. Uncle Gregory's kids call in the troops—D'Agostinos on alert. I can just see Charlie Termini (Greg's son-in-law), with his evil eye and stocky bod, preventing the younger invader from leaving the hospital lobby phone booth. "We" win the day.

I got home the next day; Stepdad was in bed with a wrenched back and an enormous nose, and he sez: "Where were you? We coulda used you."

Turns out that father and son gingerilla had bought the linoleum in another establishment. It's great to have family.

Also turns out that Uncle Gregory had his carpet knife in his back pocket during the whole conflagration. The knife was like a dagger with a forward "gut hook," and he wielded it like a black belt in linoleum trimming. He had Popeye forearms, and he could have done *real* damage. Luckily for all, the knife stayed in his back pocket.

Mom loved Uncle Gregory. He was her confidante and champion. She always left him a *macchinetta*, poised to make espresso—okay, okay, demitasse—while she was off making clothing, shopping, or visiting friends and the needy. Uncle Gregory got away with things only a brother could. For instance, during heated Vina-Lou arguments, Uncle Gregory frequently chimed in: "My brother is always right, especially when he's wrong."

Aunt Vina was very tight with Uncle Gregory's kids: three girls and a boy—Jackie, John, Tony (Antoinette), and the "baby," Connie, who was my age, and who married Charlie Termini. And these kids were *my* cousins and still are. Mom cooked many large Sunday dinners in that tiny kitchen, and our two families—and associated boyfriends/girlfriends, innamorati, and other relations dropping in all day—would eat in the store, surrounded by the vertical linoleum rolls, trying to ignore strangers knocking on the door looking for change for the laundromat next door. It was crowded, yes, but if you were spotted in the 'hood, and didn't drop in, well, don't let it happen again—I have said this elsewhere, but it bears repeating. In Mom's final struggles against the big C, *i miei cugini* (my cousins) were right there for both of us.

My brother and I worshipped Uncle Gregory. He would often open out a roll of linoleum on the wide sidewalk of 86th Street to cut and re-roll for easier delivery and installation in those walk-ups. Folks had to walk around it, and Bro' and I couldn't believe that they went by without paying homage to this great and cool man. Uncle Greg looked like Dennis Farina, the actor featured as Bones Barboni in *Get Shorty* (Barry Sonnenfeld, Director, 1995), and in TV's *Law & Order* as Detective Fontana. Even the mustaches and Sicilian backgrounds were the same. But Uncle Greg's father was not a doctor. Though powerfully built, Uncle Greg was more bent over than Farina, from a life of hard work. He had me convinced that, with his strong wrists, he could pop them over the left-field wall of Brooklyn's Ebbets Field, no problem. "Suuuure," in his vernacular.

Uncle Gregory's wife, my Aunt Millie, attended my college graduation with her sister-in-law, Vina. They were the quintessential city girls in the country—my buddies thought their observations on Ithaca, New York were hilarious. For instance: "The telephone poles are so short here;" and "The noise [crickets and amorous frogs] keeps us awake all night." At the end of her life Aunt Millie suffered from Multiple Sclerosis, and though her movements were limited, I recall her being propped up on the bed to follow the Mets, her kids tending to her. She kept her sense of humor to the end. Son-in-law Charlie told me of the time they placed her on the toilet bowl, but forgot that the cover was down—she laughed, as heartily as she could in her condition.

Uncle Gregory's oldest daughter, Jackie (named after her grandmother, probably Giacomina, of Belmonte Mezzagno) visited her Aunt Vina most Saturday afternoons, and Mom very much loved those visits. She prepared for them, in the kitchen of course. Jackie Crapanzano (her married name) had earlier been a faithful walking companion of Mom's and when long walks became difficult, cooking was the focus of their interactions, besides gossip of course.

Joseph C. Polacco

Aunt Vina also prepared for Jackie by finishing off dolls and items of clothing for grandkids, nieces, and nephews. They cooked and gossiped—*due vecchie chiacchierando* (two gossiping old ladies). Jackie even convinced Mom to go on a Caribbean cruise and a visit to New Hampshire. Uncle Gregory's kids are now all grandparents, and Aunt Vina kept track of *all* the extended family. She wrote gift checks when she didn't have the time or energy to make an outfit, doll, or blanket. It seems that the newer generations celebrate many more days than we ever did: elementary and junior high graduations, sweet sixteen…in addition to engagements, confirmations, and first communions.

Fifty years before Vina's passing, my public high school graduation ceremony was in Carnegie Hall. And Momma Vina and I took the West End to 57th Street, and then took it back to Bay Parkway, Bensonhurst. That was my graduation day, very simple, and it was lovely. As they say in the riposte to the New York Vaudeville question, "How do you get to Carnegie Hall?" "Practice, practice, practice." My agent, Vina-Mom, helped me get there.

Uncle Gregory's other kids, grandkids, and great-grandkids; were co-travelers during Mom's last fourteen-month journey. His granddaughter Charlene's "Sicilian-German" husband Richie Arent (German genes and a Sicilian stepfather), is a specialist in plumbing and installing boilers. He was a great stand-in for Mom and me, and very diplomatic in dealing with the "cascade" from the neighbors' upstairs bathroom. I like to think that when those Roman legions got bogged down trying to push back the olive oil/butter line, a war child may have been one of Richie's forebears.

Charlene reminisced just recently.

> I will never forget your mother, such a great woman, always there to help someone in need. At my wedding, after Richie and I had our first dance, my dress needed to be "bustled up." Aunt Vina, my mother [Connie], Aunt Antoinette, and my mother's co-worker helped me. They were turning

me around, and then started to tug, pin, and pull my dress together and showed me how to hold my dress. Your mother whispered to me "Remember this is your day. Smile, do not worry about anything, you look so beautiful." She danced the night away with the rest of us.

I also recall, right after my grandmother Millie died, [Aunt Vina] came over for dinner and brought her *caponatina* (cold eggplant dish), which we hadn't had in a while and all were swooning over it. After dinner Aunt Vina went to the sink to wash the dishes, and my mom said "Aunt Vina we have a dishwasher; you do not have to do that." But she wanted to. Aunt Vina went on about how much water is wasted using dishwashers and how much faster it would be if she washed at the sink. As she washed and I dried she told us about how she washed her dishes in cold water so that the people in the apartment building wouldn't run out of hot water for their showers. I always thought how selfless that was.

When my children were born she was always one of the first family to come over. She loved children and always loved to hold them and put them to sleep. After Samantha's communion she was helping Sam with her dress at the party. The last picture I have of her is from my son's communion. She is with all the Great Aunts and my Uncle John who has just passed.

Your mother was a wonderful woman; I want to be like her. A few gifts from her I will always cherish: She made my daughter Samantha a coat and booties. She made my son Richard a blanket and a yarn angel. These will be passed down and cherished always. We loved her very much.

Joseph C. Polacco

Short-lived bar in the store basement, at the end opposite my "study/lab." Left to right: Aunt Millie, Uncle John (Jijjie)—Mom's brother visiting from Las Vegas, Uncle Gregory, and Mom. 1966.

DEC 1959

Aunt Millie and Nonna Nunziatina, in our kitchen at the portal to the store.

Typical Sunday dinner in the store. Imagine that the vertical rolls of linoleum are Corinthian and Doric columns. A shade covers the front door.

Joseph C. Polacco

13. D'Agostino Clan. Pietro D'Agostino & Sons

Pietro (Peter) came over from "the other side," or Sicily, with a shovel and a work ethic. I have lost the thread of his relationship to my stepdad. He was a brother to the Giovanni-Giacomina D'Agostino marriage, and I believe on the other side of the family from the teachers' "Uncle Pete." Stepdad felt very close to Pietro, who was his uncle in any case, and I remember always having to relinquish my chair when he dropped by the back of our store. I knew I was becoming a mensch when Pietro finally noticed me, looking me in the eye as he told my stepdad that I was "getting ugly."

Pietro worked that shovel into a large trucking, excavation, and demolition company—eventually winning contracts to fill in the marshland of Gravesend Bay, thereby expanding the acreage of Bensonhurst and Bath Beach—and working on landing strips, I believe, in Vietnam. In these ventures he was joined by a rough and tumble, seemingly undisciplined, bunch of about eight sons. John, Sally, Anthony, Nascie (Ignazio), Joe, and Ronnie are the half-dozen names I recall. Think of a herd of variations on the Sylvester Stallone model. There were at least two sisters, and one married a guy from a rival family. The rivalry was more Hatfield–McCoy than Gambino–Genovese. But her spouse acted like he was mob-connected—no names please. The weddings, oh, the weddings. I thought Sally (Salvatore) on stage was a dead ringer for Frankie

Laine—another goombah, the guy who sang the *Rawhide* theme song, among other hits. Sally's renditions at weddings should have been recorded—but who had iPhones in those days? Yes, I do believe there is a genetic predisposition to gold chains and lounge lizardhood. No coincidence that Stallone rhymes with *salone*; the salone-saur (lounge lizard) never went extinct in Sicily.

I need only list a few data points to support my theory on the still-thriving salone-saurs in the modern era: Brooklyn's Julius La Rosa and Vic Damone; Bronx's Jerry Vale and Bobby Darin; Queens' Tony Bennett; Camden, NJ/Philly's Al Martino and Russ Colombo; Hoboken, NJ's Jimmy Roselli and, of course, Frank Sinatra. And, further afield, outliers from this rich fossil bed are Perry Como (Canonsburg, Pennsylvania), Dean Martin (Dino Jimmy Crocetti of Steubenville, Ohio), and Louie Prima (New Orleans).

On the topic of crooners, Mom told me of going to the Brooklyn Paramount in her youth to take in performances by Louis Prima. How did she escape my Nonna Nunziatina? She confessed that this early stage Vina was very "girlish" before her marriage at the tender age of eighteen. Prima wasn't so much a crooner, more of a bluesy gavoon from New Orleans, but a *great* entertainer. To me, he was thoroughly Brooklynized, and I present two numbers as exhibits: "Brooklyn Boogie" (composed by Earl Bostic and Louis Prima) and "Josefina, Please No Lean-a on the Bell" (composed by Duke Leonard, Ed Nelson and Harry Pease). Okay, Louis is on the Brooklyn Paramount stage, and people in the audience are eating pizza. He must have been on his third show when he says, "Sheesh, am I hungry, and that pizza smells so good. I wish I had a piece." Of course, he is bombarded by pizza. Would've been a crime if he were not. Italians don't let Italians go hungry.

Pietro lived his own life, he being of the old country. His intelligent and overlooked wife Catherine did the best she could with a brood of about ten rambunctious kids. Pietro's oldest, John, married Gussy, and they had six kids of their own. John and Pietro lived across from each other, and it seemed there was always crazy, loud "commerce" between the two households, at least when I was

Joseph C. Polacco

visiting. This family spot was on Bay 46th Street and Harway Avenue, four blocks from the famous Bay 50th Street—a real piece of Sicily, the last West End stop before Coney Island, and the starting point of the chase sequence in the film, *The French Connection*.

Now, I do not want to convey the impression that all immigrant women were under the thumbs of their husbands, many of whom had "wandering eyes." The legendary Donna Bettina was "the mayor of Bay 50th Street." Mom told me how she did a sidewalk tarantella, in high heels and summer heat, "for hours," celebrating her daughter's wedding. Donna Bettina knew everything—best to stay on her good side, 'cause she was loud, and she feared no man.

Around the corner from Gussy and Uncle Pietro was the Most Precious Blood Parish (MPB) on Bay 47th Street, just off the West End line, which at this point runs along Stillwell Avenue. The MPB summer street festival was typical—with the processional Madonna draped in dollar bills, a raised stage of fazools singing ballads from the old country, games of chance, and the aromas of freshly shucked clams, deep-fried zeppole, and sausage and pepper sandwiches. If you hit it big at roulette, the Parish Father's handshake was worth *at least* 10% of the take. These cultural treasures finally made their way into cinema in *The Godfather* (Francis Ford Coppola, Director, 1971), *Wise Guys* (Brian De Palma, Director, 1986), etcetera. *La Festa di San Gennaro* (Feast of the Patron Saint of Naples), in Little Italy, is today almost a Disney version of the real thing.

John and Gussy's family was a scaled-down version of Pietro's. In my most jealous moments, I thought that they loved Mom, and my Nonna Nunziatina, because they showed up on Sunday with lots of food. I kind of resented that, thinking they were "mortifams." *Morte di fame* literally means dying of hunger. But in usage it means someone looking to eat anything in sight, and sometimes it is meant metaphorically, as in "freeloader," "money grubber," or "mooch," or the Yiddish *schnorrer*. Gussy and family were *not* mooches in that sense. To make it worse, we not only provided good food, but I was fodder for the Sunday Bay 46th Street Yankees-inflicted torture tradition. They were Yankees fans, but their baseball "club" was really an instrument to batter me, or so it seemed to this loyal Dodger fan. And, I knew twice as much baseball as any one of them. But, the greatest insult was my losing a stickball game to Teresa, 2-1. Teresa, second oldest of John and Gussy, could have won an Olympic gold medal in basketball or softball—sheesh, in baseball for that matter. We decided to "have it out" one day, and sonuvagun; she won, fair and square. But, a poor winner she was, and she blared her glorious victory to the whole merciless gang.

As Mom always said, "Gussy has a clear head." Mom even learned how to say it in Spanish. Gussy oversaw her flock, or at least admired them as a birdwatcher might. Johnny Boy was born with little hearing. He may have lacked strong professional intervention, as far as I could tell, but I would not swear to it. However, he was not "warehoused." Rather he was extremely socialized at home, always interacting with siblings, uncles, cousins, and visitors. And he found a way to communicate—the Italian trait of speaking with hand gestures became him very well.

Mom told me of the time that Gussy had some ladies over, and Johnny Boy was deliriously happy. Gussy asked him to serve water all around, and they marveled at how cold it was. Turns out he got it from the toilet bowl—must have been winter. Gussy often sent her kids to the grocery store on Bay 46th Street—a typical hybrid neighborhood grocery store offering dry goods on the inside and fresh produce out front. One day, the designated shopper was busy, and handed the list to brother Johnny Boy, who dutifully handed it to the storekeeper. The storekeeper found the last item, "steal an onion," amusing, but the humor did not tickle his philanthropic funny bone.

Gussy always thought me square—but I can't be defined as some regular and symmetrical geometrical figure. I had to be the only guy in Brooklyn to get married in a Quaker meeting house—in Westbury, Long Island—and have the reception at the Villa Vivolo in Bensonhurst. Uncle Gregory knew how to find the meeting

Joseph C. Polacco

house 'cause it was near a favorite racetrack. And the Villa Vivolo became easier to find, some months later, via Gael Greene's *New York* magazine restaurant column of April 7, 1969—"the Mafia Guide to Dining Out." The gist of her article was that when Mafia "sit-downs" were raided by the police, the restaurant became de rigueur for "foodies." (Not a 1969 word, which I hate. Gussy would have given me a well-deserved dope slap if I had used it. She'd a whacked me if I invented it.)

Okay, at the Villa Vivolo, Gussy looks at me across the room, and paints an air-square with her two forefingers. I don't recall my transgression—maybe I wouldn't go out drinking with her on my wedding night.

Mom seemed to enjoy Gussy's company, or perhaps she was drawn to her because she felt for the kids. I know Mom felt sorry for Teresa, because she was not getting due respect and support from her uncles and cousins, who were always around, mind you. For example, Teresa fell in love with the sax, and played a rendition for them one Sunday. They awaited her with cups of ice water, not the Super Bowl victory kind. I could not believe that she actually cried in my presence, and confided in me, "They don't let you do shit around here." Mom understood. Oh, did she understand. Teresa knew it and stayed tight with Mom, her Aunt Vina, for the rest of Mom's life. At the famous D'Agostino family reunion impromptu softball game, Teresa told me, "Joe, you put the hard tag on that little snot like a real D'Agostino." Such gems sparkle along my life path. But it was Mom who helped Teresa, me, and others forge the paths of our own choosing.

My bro' and I were madly in love with Marie D'Agostino, bride of Sally (son of Pietro and Catherine), and Gussy's sister-in-law. Now, Sally was one of the more "serious" brothers, good at bookkeeping and managing the business. Yes, he was a lounge lizard, and yes, he fooled around on the side. But, he was responsible and smart, and he had Marie, his forbearing, beautiful, intelligent, and perspicacious wife. She was a Barese-Napoletana, just like me. She was always a center of attention at the many D'Agostino wedding galas.

Sally has long been gone, and Marie is holding on to the house her father built on Bay 47th Street and Stillwell Avenue. Until her health recently declined, she worked the garden every year, cherishing the plastic holders of her dad's guinea stinkers in the turned soil—they are still there. She was hit very hard by Superstorm Sandy, but her good brothers brought the house back to life. The garden, hit by sewage, oil, gasoline—well, another story. Marie has fifty-six nieces/nephews and grand-nieces/nephews, but no kids. Sally had one with his second wife. Marie truly loved Mom, and felt very guilty about Mom falling on the steps that her dad built. Marie, it was *not* your fault.

I find silly things precious—like Marie's Friday afternoon ritual of visiting the beauty parlor near Mom's apartment. When in town, I braved the atmosphere of solvent and hair spray to sit with the ladies and enjoy the gossip. Vina was always there, of course, and sometimes even had her hair done. The place was run by a Jewish woman, but the Italian and Jewish clientele were like a throwback to the old days—days that Mom cherished, and so do I, for that matter.

Marie is great at kvetching, and life has given her great material. Just one example: when I made it back, eventually, from Spain to accompany Mom to Maimonides for her lumpectomy in 2004, Marie drove us. Now, Marie's circulatory problems mean that her feet are very painful, so she needs to find a parking place near the hospital. Finally, she finds a place. Then, as she would say it, "I get all these summonses, and notices, and bills, and threats to have my license revoked. And why? Some *stunad* switched my plates—I have plates from a stolen car, and he uses mine, and parks wherever he damn pleases. Sonuvabitch, just my rotten luck."

By the way, stunad is "stupid." It's often used in self-deprecation, as in, "Sometimes, I wake up stunad." It can also mean brain stupor, as in, "Tony, shut up already with the Mets; you're making me stunad!" Repetitive insults to one's sanity also evoke the beautiful camurria.

Donna Bettina. The back of this photo is handwritten in Italian. While not too legible, it is definitely signed "Baci, Bettina." I love the enduring strength in this woman's countenance.

Photos courtesy Polacco family

Vina and Marie, at the house built by Marie's beloved father. Marie passed in early 2016.

14. Food is Love

"I think about Noni every time I cook or run out of olive oil."

—*My first wife, Mary Schaeffer, on her former mother-in-law*

Food was double love for me, and for all doted-on kids whose loving mothers love to cook. And, just as was true for many children of my generation, the dishes were also a connection to my grandmother, and to the old country. I did not realize how lucky we of the Brooklyn "ethnic" generations were. The "American" moms June Cleaver (the Beav's mom) and Harriet Nelson (Ricky's mom) made casseroles and roasts, while I was being served eggplant *parmigiano*, *spidini*, and *finocchio e sarde*. (Brooklyn not only lost the Dodgers to Los Angeles, but our food was oh so retro as well. I *almost* felt deprived, but got smart real soon. At the time I did not see the irony in Hollywood proffering Italian food and customs in their blockbusters, such as *The Godfather*.)

Finocchio e sarde is a fennel and sardine sauce. In dialect, it was elided into one word: "finokiaSOD." This Sicilian dish takes acclimation, but is definitely fortifying served over pasta. You can recognize the fish remains, and the greenish finocchio—the bulb and the aerial fronds are used, but not the fennel seeds. The seeds are used in other foods, salsiccia for instance. Pine nuts and raisins are

Joseph C. Polacco

reminders that this is a Mediterranean dish, and those ingredients were probably enjoyed by Archimides in the third century BCE.

Spidini—ahhhh, *lots* of work, but a real treat—are basically rolled veal or beef filled with bread crumbs and herbs. They can be skewered and grilled. Mom placed them upright in a pan and baked them—each one a little treasure. *Braccioli* (brazhole) are larger meat rolls, filled with *pignolia* (pine nuts), grated cheese, parsley, and garlic. They are more loosely rolled and held together with toothpicks (careful!), and are usually cooked in a *ragú* (tomato meat sauce), but not the store-bought kind. Co-habitants of the murky ragú depths were often meatballs, salsiccie, and *cútana* (pig's knuckles, feet, jowls, etcetera). I have no idea how cútana is spelled, but think "cutaneous;" the porcine epidermis sheds its goodness in the long-simmering sauce. Some folks remove the feet before serving. Mom avoided feet all the time—no feet on *her* table.

Mom and Nonna Nunziatina could *cook*, but they did not follow the American tradition of baking. With the exception of Christmas *struffoli* (honey balls) and a few other items, like a really heavy cheesecake and *pizza rústica*, they didn't have to. The *pasticceria* (pastry shop), was usually a block or so away, and the bakers/pastry chefs often earned their U.S. citizenship by dint of their mastery of the arcane craft. Mom said that many took their trade secrets to the grave. I suppose this stimulated issuance of more green cards.

I recall being sent to the pastry shop to pick up *sfogliatelle*, cannoli, and *rum babá*. I was too embarrassed to ask for the latter; what an idiot I was. There were two shops about two short blocks from our home, DiFillippi's and Reliable: biscotti, zeppole, sfingi, cuccidati—the list goes on. Bread? Outtadisworld; don't get me started. Mr. DiFillippi had a couple of beautiful daughters who were my age, and I loved when they came out of the back to serve the clientele. Their dark complexions gently smudged with flour, matching their white aprons, were a combined celestial cosmetological and culinary gift that was not lost on me. Many pasticcerie also made pizza; in fact, the dedicated pizzeria was not that common back in the day.

This is not a cookbook, but I wanted to transcribe some cooking tips from Vina in her own voice—tips interspersed with commentary and, yes, gossip. She had all kinds of weird inventions, such as *bicchia bacchia* sauce (pine nuts, raisins, etcetera)—does this exist anywhere out there? Transcription is difficult, because her recipes came with sidebars such as, "So-and-so puts too much salt in it, and she has pressure," or "The Sicilians laugh at you if you leave the [pecorino] cheese out of the meatballs." And then, she's off on a tangent.

Okay, I'm my mother's son, and here is a tangent: Bensonhurst medical terminology can be quaint. You have probably guessed that "she has pressure" means "she has high blood pressure." A shot/vaccination at the doctor's office is "getting a needle," and, while you can be diabetic, you usually "have sugar." Acid indigestion is *ágita*, treated with Brioschi, the effervescent Italian antacid. Somehow, all of the above are related to food, and all are both Italian and non-Italian expressions in Bensonhurst. Oh yes, "you have a temperature" means you have a fever.

Some of Vina's recipes are for historical sake because, for instance, I wasn't going to make *sanguinaccio, figado maiale,* or *sticchioli*. I wrote much of the following in shorthand during a phone conversation with Mom. Sanguinaccio is pig's blood pudding, also with chocolate, citron, nuts, sugar, among other ingredients mixed into a homogeneous blend, not to be done too fast, but before blood starts to rise on the wooden spoon by capillary action and later coagulate. Heavy cream, drizzled in at the end, finishes it off. This confection is a real art, and is quite good, actually, but where do you get pig's blood in Brooklyn now? Figado maiale is young porker's liver wrapped with a "veil of peritoneum," which is the best I can come up with, and for which I believe the dialect is *arezza*. Sticchioli, typically Barese, is lamb intestine, split and washed well in brine and water, garnished with bay leaf, and grilled. Now, I learned of the Uruguayan version of this from my Nancy: Their version, *chinchulín*, is made of beef intestine, and is still served at *asados* (home barbecues) and the best *churrasquerías*—those lovely restaurants where an inferno of grilling beef, chorizo, chicken, red bell peppers, melted provolone, and other wonderful delights greets you; especially welcoming on cold nights.

We Americans have lost our zest for organ meats. In the 'hood back in the day, *vastedda* (Vah-SHTED in dialect) used to be sliced cow lung, served on a lovely sesame seed roll slathered with olive oil, garlic, ricotta (lots), and a grated sharp cheese, usually *caciocavallo* (literally "horse cheese," but not from mare's milk). This was a great hot treat on a cold day. Now, to comply with health codes, another meat is used, and Google tells me that it's beef spleen, so we are not in a complete cultural wasteland.

I realize that I am dwelling almost exclusively on Italian foods. As I have mentioned, Jewish and Chinese food was available all over the Bensonhurst of my youth. Expand that now to Mexican, Central American, Turkish, Greek, Russian, Egyptian, Vietnamese, Japanese, ad infinitum (but not ad nauseam). So back in the day, when we did not go Italian or Chinese, we went Jewish. And, I still can't visit the 'hood without my taste buds and nose being tempted by:

Knishes—A more sophisticated cousin of the latke potato pancake. Knishes are baked with garlic, eggs, salt, and pepper—how could you go wrong, especially on cold nights?

Pastrami—on rye/pumpernickel with a kosher dill.

Kosher hotdogs—No comment necessary. They beat out ballpark franks, and I don't think Nathan's Famous in Coney Island (now franchised, oy) serves these. Then again—blasphemy—shove kosher dogs down the craw to win some kind of orgiastic contest on the Fourth of July?! What are you, meshuggenah?

Kosher salami—DON'T hold the garlic.

Challah—A braided, rich bread, with eggs, oil, and some sugar mixed into the dough. If you didn't have a wet, guttural "Ch," they wouldn't serve you in Schlom and Deutch bakery on 86th Street (well, they would, out of pity). Billy Crystal said that Yiddish is basically equal parts German and phlegm.

Bialys—Standard fare in Schlom and Deutch, and in bagel emporia everywhere. Kind of like soft-hearted bagels, not nearly as chewy, and with a depression in the middle lovingly and subtly appointed with caramelized onions. I thought they acquired their name from "white" flour (as in Beloruss for White Russia), but they are named after their origin: Bialystok, Poland. Uruguayan Nancy always brought a couple of packs back to Missouri from Brooklyn.

Hamentaschen—I mentioned these filled, baked wonders in Chapter 1. From my Columbia, Missouri neighbor, Tim Parshall: "[They are filled with] prune, apple, cherry, apricot...all are delightful, but my favorite filling is a poppy-seed spread, thick enough that those subject to drug testing are rumored to have failed after consuming one!"

Onion Boards—America is now officially in love with bagels. They are as much a part of our cuisine as pizza—calzone is not very far behind. Even "back in the day" there were special bagel joints, and one just a block from our store on 86th Street. There was a much larger place, on or near 18th Avenue. It supplied bakeries, delis, and smaller retail outlets. Early Sunday mornings, as I tried to schlep my "challenged" bike to the Journal-American office to pick up papers for my home delivery route, the aroma emanating from that place gave this little *goy* the strength to push on. Part of that aroma was the onion board—as close to Jewish focaccia as I can imagine.

Mom's friend Lily de Candia was a very brassy character, even for the 'hood. She and Mom had occasion to walk by the bagel bakey place almost daily, perhaps from a nearby sweat shop. Lily always tried to mooch a bagel or two. But one day, she had the audacity to ask for an onion board. The long-suffering guy would always give her a few bagels. But the onion board? Well, he resisted some, and Lily comes at him with, "I'm pregnant" (not). In no way buying her assertion, he gives her that resigned Yiddish look—*yes*, Yiddish is not only a spoken language, it is also body language and facial gestures, and this guy had the accent too. "Oy, so you're pregnant? Here, take this, and best of luck with the baby." This was a much lighter version of the mob shaking down small business owners. Lily was large, loud, and thoroughly entertaining. Her daughters Patrina and Lucille were my buddies.

But, I have to add that I never really got hooked on gefilte fish. Perhaps I did not know the right people. I think, as the Italians say, you have to grow up *nella miseria*—in the depths of poverty—to appreciate survival food. And, though I loved Mom's matzoh ball soup, I never got into matzoh. I suppose you have to grow up with unleavened bread, and make associations to family and holidays. My Jewish schoolmates ate buttered matzoh. Oy, unleavened doesn't mean fat-free. I won't go near Manischewitz wine; my wine has to be dry, molto secco—yes, I'm a wine snob. Then again, I never tried dunking buttered matzoh in Manischewitz—could be a verse in "Moon over Miami" (Manna in Milwaukee?).

So, with all the intermarriage, commerce, and joint ventures, at least in Bensonhurst, could there not have been Jewish-Italian crossover? Well, there is also a long, oft-tragic history of Jews living in Italy. After all, *ghetto* is from the Italian. As with many in the peninsula, they endured la miseria, and found kindred plants that were also hardy and opportunistic—and nourishing. I refer specifically to the artichoke—*acacciofa*, as it sounded to me, carciofo in the dictionary. As the story went, Jews found it by the arid roadsides, and learned how to prepare and possibly cultivate it. I told this story to Mom, and she was in *no* mood to accept its validity. In truth, acacciofa has a reverent status in the cucina italiana; not sure it was as popular with my Jewish friends. Joe Valachi, one of the first mob informants, talked about mobster Ciro Terranova cornering the artichoke market and becoming rich as "The Artichoke King" because, and I paraphrase from Peter Maas' 1968 Book, *The Valachi Papers*: "Italians *got* to have artichokes to eat." Word of cheap and good artichokes on 86th Street spread like wildfire among the donne, including Julie, of Bensonhurst.

My Bensonhurst baseball and bug buddy, Peter Lamontia reminded me of an early introduction to Jewish cooking: "When I was ten or eleven I had a friend, Bruce Rabinowitz, who lived on Bay Parkway. He invited me in for breakfast one early morning when I arrived at his house to ask him out to play." [We did that in the old days; we "called for someone to come out and play."] Inside, his mother asked me to sit down and have some mashed potatoes and sour cream for breakfast—*what*?! My first experience in Jewish cuisine. I winced, but to tell you the truth, I actually liked it."

So, the previous paragraph reminds me that we did not have to go to restaurants to experience the food of "the other." We were often guests at each other's tables. And *Brooklyn* (both the novel by Colm Tóibín and the 2015 movie, John Crowley, Director) recalls that Mom's youth was, if not immersed in Irish culture, certainly confronted by it. The Italians were the "next wave" after the Irish, who had sewn up the unions representing the police and firemen (now fire*fighters*). But, the dagos became strong in the sanitation workers union. Yes, I can see derisive smirks, but a garbage collection strike is a fearful thing, almost a Weapon of Mass Destruction.

Brother Michael witnessed was at a St. Patty's Day parade during which many of the spectators were, well, inebriated. No surprise there, but when the sanitation crew followed the last of the marchers, there rose a cry from among the viewers, "And here come the Italians!" Michael witnessed a Wall Street type with Mediterranean features slam an offending celebrant over the head with his attaché case. Our "honor" was upheld that day.

Times were good before the depression really took hold. Mom's grandfather, Giovanni Rainone, bought a house on Van Sicklen Street in the Gravesend section of Brooklyn, amidst many Irish families. The Saints Simon and Jude neighborhood parish had a school staffed mainly by Irish nuns. Margaret married Mom's uncle Mario (mentioned in the dialog below). Margaret was an "Americanized" Italian who picked up a "retro" Italian accent from husband Mario and sister-in-law Nunziatina, who lived nearby with Vina, Vina's siblings and, eventually, her mother when she was widowed from Giovanni Rainone.

Margaret entertained neighborhood Irish kids at meal times. One lunch at Aunt Margaret's featured lentil soup. The Irish guest, a lass of probably eleven, asked what it was, and got the answer: "Fly soup." The lentils, when partially opened, could be imagined to look like flies. Later that afternoon, she excitedly told her mom, Mrs. Flynn: "Momma, I had fly soup at Mrs. Rainone's!" We had the luck o' the Irish, because Mrs. Flynn had a sense of humor.

I recorded Mom over the last five months of her life as we chatted at the kitchen table. Of course, I did not know, at least not at first, how close she was to the end. Our conversations in the beginning were more upbeat; the first chemo regime seemed to be working. So, I used recipes as a pretext for recording, and we talked food at the table—to the percussive sounds of utensils hitting my plate, and food my palate. Mom was usually running between the table and the stove, fridge, or sink.

Parts of an early conversation:

The recording just kicks in to laughter, and I will never know what brought it on.

> *Joe:* Grounds for divorce. [I *think* this was about a woman who left her husband because all he wanted to eat was pasta.]
>
> *Mom:* I'm looking at him, and saying: "Is he for real?"
>
> *Joe:* I hadn't heard the story about [a female, with a familiar name]. So that, I mean, she took him to…I mean she divorced him; I mean, that was a *legal* reason?
>
> *Mom:* She didn't want him anymore.
>
> *Joe:* I mean, it was like cruel and unusual *punishment*?
>
> *Mom:* She said, "You know what? We must call it a day."
>
> [Laughter both]
>
> *Mom:* If the man was a poor man, and even though, you gotta dirty a pot anyway. What do you say to him?

Was dirtying a pot metaphorical? Then we get into culinary veritás. As mentioned above, Mario was Nonna Nunziatina's brother. He, his wife Margaret, and their family moved to Chicago, where they opened an Italian restaurant.

Mom: You know what they do in restaurants? My uncle Mario showed me. Uncle Mario made lots of macaroni. He put it in the *scolapasta* [strainer] already done, with oil, on top of boiling water; but a lot of restaurants do that. People want their clams and macaroni.

Today we'd say the oh-so-continental, *linguine alle vongole.*

Mom: He puts it on top of the scolapasta. [Whispered:] They used a lot of gas.
Joe: Well, you gotta boil a lot of water, but still…
Mom: They *do* boil a lot of macaroni.
Joe: They seal it in Ziploc bags, right?
Mom: Nope.
Joe: The spaghetti is already done?
Mom: The spaghetti is already done. It's already done.

And then Mom repeats the procedure for my *capo dost,* or thick head.

Mom: But a lot of restaurants do that.
Joe: Huh. You know how the Cajuns make pasta? The Cajuns, you know, New Orleans. They like a lot of pasta.

I have left this long discourse out of the transcript. It describes partially-cooked Cajun pasta being chilled, and then coated in oil. It is "finished off" by sucking up the spicy seafood juices of their concoctions. Heavenly, really, but planning well is important because I always feel obliged to eat all the pasta in one sitting.

Joseph C. Polacco

> *Mom:* I had a lot of juice in my clams and macaroni. [Joe grunts.] Joseph, eat the meatballs. Here's a spoon.
>
> *Joe:* How come you're sitting over there? Because you knew I was going to record you, that's why.
>
> *Mom:* No [soft, plaintive].
>
> [Lots of slurping.]
>
> *Mom:* Sit up straight Jogie Wogie.

She called me by my baby name, which came from a WWII song about a Japanese spy—Jogie Wogie. Also note that Mom, dealing with cancer and chemo, wants me to sit up straight, for my own well-being.

Then followed Mom's advice on *bruschetta* and *casiolo*—the latter a baked version of squash, with eggs, onions, and cheese. I was going to provide details, but the descriptions are "fractured." I will be happy to try to answer personal requests.

Mom, who could speak at least two Italian dialects, and Brooklynese like the native she was, had a few problems with Spanish. To Mom, adobo was "adooba." She loved adobo as a salt substitute. Mom had a "thing" about salt, and at almost every meal I would hear, "And, I put no salt in it."

Our talk about food turned to Frank McCourt. Mom was deeply impressed with his book *Angela's Ashes*. She felt a connection to McCourt, probably because she went to school with the Irish and most of her teachers were Irish nuns. Indeed, McCourt taught English at Stuyvesant, my public high school at the end of his teaching career. Mom also loved his book *Teacher Man* which describes the life of a teacher.

> *Mom:* Joseph, he ate garbage; his mother lost a baby from starvation before he was born. He ate garbage—bread with sugar—look at the brain on him. Came to the U.S.A. 1948, at eighteen years old.

[Actually, McCourt was born in Brooklyn, and his family returned to Limerick, Ireland, before he went back to New York. He worked the docks by day, while earning his teaching degree at NYU, mostly in the evening.]

> *Joe:* Still alive?
> *Mom:* Noo, he died. He was the puniest brother of the bunch—runt of the litter.
> *Joe:* That's what they used to say about Robert Kennedy. Our kids are just the opposite. They'll be dying from malnutrition because of eating too much salt, sugar, fat.

Again, I leave out the transcript, in which I became professorial: about how half of our younger generation, and two out of three minority kids will eventually suffer from malnutrition. Of course, I was just recounting what an exercise physiologist was maintaining in a public lecture. Then I went off on Pima Indians having an exceedingly high incidence of cardiovascular disease, probably as a result of many generations of selection for getting the most nutrition out of poor and low-calorie diets.

> *Mom:* See, the slaves ate crap. They ate the worst—all the gristle ["grizzle"], fat. How come they never had any problem?
> *Joe:* Ahhh, but they did. They died young, and there had to be a selection involved; not just physical, but psychological.

Another interlude on West Indian employees at the home (Jamaicans, et al.) being overweight and diabetic, and yet eating sweets.

> *Mom:* How does that taste [the robbies]? I bought frozen broccoli raab; Joseph, never again. Seabrook.
> *Joe:* Like Birds Eye? Was it prepared?

Mom: Terrible—all water and stalks. I told Anna [Uncle Mario and Aunt Margaret's daughter], "*Don't buy it!*" But, I made this myself. Was it good?

Joe: It was good. [Notice the past tense.]

Mom: Finish the bread.

Joe: I finished it; I tried some of the lard bread that was still left.

Mom: Jackie, she *loves* that bread.

Joe: So does Nancy.

Mom: The week before, [Jackie] ate almost a whole loaf!

[Laughter]

Lard bread is one of a group of peasant delicacies—oxymoron intended. My Nonna Nunziatina used to ask the butcher to grind leftover ends of salami, prosciutto, soppressata, etcetera, and then she would bake them into lard bread. Grandma *always* accused the butcher of "skimming." "His family is going to eat well tonight!" At times, she went a step further, to the *really* fat-indulgent *pizza rustica*—pie with extra eggs, ricotta, mozzarella, sausage, etcetera.

Mom: See, I'm okay. I lost a lot of desires. I lost desire for coffee, chocolate, and bread.

Joe: It's coming back. [I said this with hope in my heart.]

Mom: I don't want it to come back.

Joe: No, not that the desire is good; it's just what it means.

[A pause in which dishes and silverware are clanking.]

Mom: I got more meatballs in there, and I got more pasta in there. You know when I went to Filomena's house, she made a whole pound—that's a *lot* for three people.

Joe: Stevie [her son] didn't have any?

Mom: Sure [*sotto voce*].

Joe: Well, that's four people, maybe five.

I'm such a comedian. Then follows an interlude on the guy's eating habits—a guy who should know better, what with a heart stent.

Mom: He's pretty young. How are the meatballs?

Joe: Gooood.

Mom: I don't put cheese in it.

Joe: I was talking with Nancy, and she heard me say meatballs, or something. And, "Oh, your mother's meatballs!"

Mom: I stopped with cheese a long, long time ago [completely ignoring my relayed praise from Nancy]. And I don't tell anybody, 'cause they make fun of you, especially the Sicilians: "How could you make meatballs without cheese?!" There's fennel in here too.

Joe: Hmmm. Is there sausage in here also?

Mom: Pork and beef.

Joe: So the fennel came with the pork.

Mom: From the pork. Julie doesn't like fennel.

Joe: Hey, to each his own. He must *hate* finocchio e sarde [hee hee].

Mom: But, he likes to eat everything *rich*. Everything with mozzarella, ricotta, mozzarella, ricotta, formaggio, mozzarella, ricotta…*everything*. Like, I was telling him I was making a *frittata*, and he sez, "Why don't you put some mozzarella in it?" "Why?" I said, "I've got the cheese and the eggs, that's enough." I said, "No."

Mom: I'm so proud of Jackie. Poor kid, she's got pains.

Mom: And I've got [wal]nuts in there, but you don't see them. I ground them very, very thin, so you don't see them. I put them in the chopper.

Joe: I saw a couple. I see 'em, Ma. [Mom was saving money not using pine nuts, especially since the ones from Italy cost an arm and a leg—even in the "Casbah" stores of 86th Street—and the ones from China are "too cheap."]

Mom: And, I don't put bread crumbs in there; I put bread.

Joe: Jackie is seventy-seven?

Mom: She's seventy-six; she's eleven years younger than me.

Joe: Back in the day, those eleven years made a big difference. Well, now they do, too. [How profound I am, *non è vero?*]

Mom: Ohh, are you kidding? Joseph, could I do what I did five years ago? Never! Look how tired I was yesterday. Joseph, I was ashamed of myself.

Joe: Ma, Ma, nothing to be ashamed about, Ma! [A little guilt was speaking here.]

Mom: Maronna, was I tired!

Enough scattershot conversation. The more I listen, the more I realize the sacrifices she made for my visits, visits that were supposed to help her in her struggle. Conversations got "darker" with time, and the transcription is difficult for me, because it was obvious I was not reading the intended meaning of many of her utterances (or I did not want to). For instance, "I'm trying to talk away from what I'm thinking."

And, I will talk this conversation back to cooking. Jackie Crapanzano always thinks of her Aunt Vina when she cooks garlic. Mom went through enough garlic in her lifetime to keep a Romania full of Lugosi's at bay. *And,* she *never* burned garlic. She avoided this mortal sin by heating garlic in the skillet in an olive oil/water mix. The boiling water heats the oil, which extracts the goodness of the garlic without getting super hot. (Thanks, Mom, for my Chemistry 101 genes.)

Before the water is gone, and garlic burns, she adds the rest of the ingredients—for example, broccoli di rapa. Aside: No one matches the Vina mania for cleaning robbies, and the result was, and still is, the best I have had, anywhere. Back to garlic: For me, the oil/water technique is not easy, and I often have to fend off "spitting oil." For each misstep, I hear Mom over my shoulder: "Don't burn the garlic!" I wonder if bad garlic burns in hell.

It is obvious that one center of Mom's universe was the kitchen (duhhh); first behind the store, then above it, and finally, in her apartment on 77th Street and 21st Avenue—all small, but each her sorcerer's working space. And, though generous, she was not prosperous, and her good Italian heart was matched by steely Yankee thrift. I think Ben Franklin said, "No revenue is secure without *economy*." So, though she used an OPEC quantity of olive oil, *rarely* did I see her use *stra vergine*, or extra virgin oil. She bought her oil in one of the "Casbah" stores on 86th Street—keeping an eagle eye out for the best deal. The two wheels on her shopping cart should have had a maintenance agreement. Remember, nine "street" blocks and two "avenue" blocks to the stores, in all kinds of weather, back and forth. And, she schlepped her cart up twenty-two steps to her apartment.

Almost as pleasurable as cooking for Mom, was to save a few bucks on oil, robbies, artichokes, pasta, whatever. If I paid $1.59/lb for robbies, instead of $1.39 "at the Koreans," she blew a gasket. She walked eleven blocks for those kinds of savings. Prepared foods? Ma quando? Mai! Giving in to them was a sure sign that she was seriously ill.

Now, I have to go to my native tongue when I say: "Not for nuthin' but prepared foods in da 'hood, Maronna mia, are da high-quality stuff." Such as *insalata di mare* (seafood salad), or veal parmigiano, offered by Pastosa Ravioli Company on New Utrecht Avenue, or Leoni's on 15th Avenue, or the 86th Street Meats Supreme (a name that only Brooklyn would deem normal), and many more. Go ahead, Google them, I dare you.

I would be remiss not to convey a couple of recipes. A few years back, over the phone, I was able to pin Mom down and get her advice for shrimp scampi. Cooking advice is best received while cooking, so that we both stay focused. I followed her recipe many times, but, as is true of scientific procedures, and probably the retelling of stories, the recipe "evolves" over time.

Mom's Shrimp Scampi recipe:

Ingredients

- Three pounds medium-sized shrimp, shelled and deveined (You can get away with two, but this keeps really well as frozen leftovers.)
- Half-cup dry white wine
- Half-cup seafood stock (see "Observations" below.)
- ¾ bunch parsley, split in two portions (½ and ¼) and diced (You can use a lot of the upper stem and petioles.)
- 8-10 large, healthy, smelly garlic cloves (or more, if you're me)
- Bread crumbs (can be store-bought and seasoned, but not necessary 'cause you will season it yourself)
- A "pinch," according to taste, of either cayenne pepper or Cajun-style spice (My Cajun spice is based on Paul Prud-homme's 1989 book on Louisiana cooking. I modified by halving the amount of salt. No, no added "adooba.")
- 4 tsp dry parsley
- Olive oil (enough to cover the bottom of a small frying pan, and maybe a little more)—stra vergine, *certo*

1. Get the oven to 375° F.
2. Mince/press garlic and add to deep frying pan with olive oil. Start to heat on medium, <u>taking care not to brown the garlic</u> (using, of course, Mom's trick to add a little water, so that, as it starts to boil, the garlic is "shielded," and its goodness is ex-tracted by the oil. Add a little more water as needed).
3. Add the shrimp, and sprinkle with Cajun spice. *Cook only partially*. Add the dried parsley, the ½ bunch of minced fresh parsley, the seafood stock, and the white wine.

4. Cook just a little further—*the shrimp should be only partially done.*

5. Add the whole mixture to a ceramic "casserole" dish. (Thanks, June Cleaver.)

6. Cover shrimp with a layer of bread crumbs that have previously been mixed with a little Cajun spice to taste, a little dried parsley, and the rest of the minced fresh parsley (do not overdo the latter). This layer should not be "wet," though portions will look so.

7. Cover and bake at 375° F for about 30 minutes. (Check on it to make sure shrimp are cooked.) At times, I remove the cover and broil for another 5 minutes to make the surface more *croccante*, or crispy.

Observations:

• I like to serve this with Basmati rice on the side—the tangy shrimp goes well with the rice. Steamed broccoli completes the beauty of the dish. And, of course, it goes well with a good, deep-bodied red wine (Chianti, Cabernet-Sauvignon, Argentine Malbec, or Uruguayan Tannat).

• Anointing the shrimp with lemon juice is optional, an option I prefer.

• The shrimp "renderings" are fantastic when sopped up with good Italian semolina bread.

Notes on Seafood stock:

Like Mom, I use the liquor that exudes from the shrimp, but also have made my own stock—often by boiling the shells. When Mom visited me in Spain, we learned that bones of *gallo* made a great stock. Gallo, rooster, is also the name given to a lovely large flounder. It was available fresh daily, and was filleted in front of us at the market. The fishmongers knew the bones of which fish made the best *caldo*. Mom, watching the guy fillet, said: "There is a man who loves his work." Other components can go into stock, mussel and clam shells, for instance. Spanish shrimp came with heads on, and I confess that the heads made an evilly good stock. Now I use a commercial concentrated stock. Penzeys Spices offers an excellent product; indeed, they reproduced this recipe on their website.

Vina's Potato Pizza

Gayle Olinekova included Mom's potato pizza recipe in her 1982 book *Go For It!* (Simon and Schuster New York, A Fireside Book). The book was a guide to good living, the right exercises and, of course, good eating. I reproduce the recipe here:

> At one point in my life, I carried only two telephone numbers in my wallet in case of emergency—my lawyer's and the pizzeria's.
>
> Pizza was a powerful addiction to overcome in subsequent years of food reform, yet I still submit to it in New York City, where Vina D'Agostino, an accomplished Italian gourmet chef, never fails to delight me with this original recipe.

Ingredients
- 3 lb potatoes
- 2 tbsp olive oil or butter
- 2 eggs
- 1 lb mozzarella cheese
- 2 tbsp fresh parseley (or 1 tbsp dry)
- 1 tsp oregano
- Resting on your Laurels Tomato sauce to taste (Joe's note: This sauce is a Gayle creation, and is made from fresh, peeled plum tomatoes, garlic, fresh basil, bay leaves and olive oil—how bad can it be? I agree with Gayle—the simpler the better, though I sometimes use olive oil that was used to sautée onions, but lightly [Mom's trick], and some tomato paste for body.)

1. Scrub potatoes with a veggie brush. Quarter and drop them in boiling water—just enough to barely cover. After cooking, discard water, and mash.
2. In a separate bowl, beat two eggs with parsley. Add to potatoes with olive oil and mix well.
3. Spread potato mixture on lightly oiled pizza pan very thinly, pressing with palms of hands to one-half-inch thickness.
4. Bake in a hot oven (400° F) until golden brown.
5. Slice or shred fresh mozzarella to desired taste onto crust. Add tomato sauce and re-insert in oven for five minutes. Then remove, and put remaining mozzarella on top. Shut off oven and re-insert to melt cheese. Sprinkle oregano lightly, and serve.

Feeds: two pizza addicts—four athletes—six polite guests.

Mom with first cousin Anna Harris in upstairs kitchen.
Anna is daughter of Mario, sister of Nonna Nunziatina.

Mom in our back-of-store kitchen. Note the size and relative inaccessibility. There was a bathroom sink, and we used the bathroom at times for cooking. I recall a pot of snails in the bathtub—the lid was to be "ajar" to allow light to enter, thus encouraging the snails to emerge from their shells. After playing with them for a while, I forgot to put the cover back on, and we wound up pulling our dinner off the walls of the tub and the bathroom.

Mom in kitchen of 77th Street apartment. Georgette and Toni helped Mom get the new fridge via a City of New York program to replace old fridges with more energy-efficient new ones.

Nonna Nunziatina with her mother Magherita, and brother Mario. The kitchen was on Avenue T and West 6th Street. All were born in Italy. Great-grandma had trouble living without Mediterranean sunshine, but she made it to age eighty-eight, having spent half her life in America.

Photos courtesy Polacco family

Photos courtesy Toni Caggiano

This example of Toni Caggiano's 2016 Easter baking really brings home that food is love, and that it links generations. The top, round cake, is Vina's cheese cake, complete with orange zest. (I tended to sit on my Nonna's cheese cakes—she would leave them on seats to cool.) The square cake is Large Mary's Pizza Rustica—I can still picture her, scissors in hand, cutting pieces of cheese, pepperoni, prosciutto, while she kept us enthralled with stories. The smaller rounds are "Easter Breads" for grandkids and neighbors. They are supposed to represent birds' nests, complete with an egg—now back after being considered taboo when Toni's kids were young. The young-uns eventually do come around.

15. The Neighborhood Changes

The interior 'hoods of Brooklyn continue to be the same, constantly stirring minestrone/*estofado*/*stracciatella*/stew, but with ever-new ingredients. The outer 'hoods, the ones near the Brooklyn Bridge and Prospect Park, appear to be increasingly populated by a "reverse migration" of professionals and millennials from the American frontier—"smart," Vina would say. By the time of Mom's passing in early 2013, even interior Bensonhurst had very much changed from the Bensonhurst of my youth. This change was more ethnic—another word I sometimes deplore. What makes something ethnic—dark skin? A non-European language? Non-Judeo-Christian beliefs?

So, *all* New York neighborhoods constantly evolve, no matter the new ingredients. I was born on Our Lady of Mt. Carmel day—hence my middle name, Carmine—a Hollywood mobster name. And near the eponymous church on East 116th Street, in what used to be the Italian Harlem of Mario Puzo (and Joe Valachi), immigrant Italians had to take their "ebullient" celebrations and processions indoors, because they were too over-the-top for the previous generations of immigrants, mostly Irish. Though that neighborhood now includes much of "Spanish Harlem," a few Italians remain on Pleasant Avenue. Still hanging on in Brooklyn's Williamsburg section is the *Festa del Giglio* (the "Feast of the Lily"). On or around my birthday, July 16, this festival also occurs in Italy.

Sicilian versus Neapolitan was a big rivalry in the Bensonhurst of my youth. Sicilians had *la cosa nostra*, and Neapolitans *la camorra*, but the differences were deeper and broader than that. Mom told a story about a Sicilian woman—I don't recall her *paese*—with four sons. Three married Sicilian girls, but the fourth married a Napoletana—aii, che peccato! (In this usage peccato is more of a sin than a pity.) Mother-in-law told Mom that this girl was *da un'altro pianeta* (from another planet)! And she says this knowing full well that Mom is Napoletana, a Napoletana speaking her Sicilian dialect, fercryinoutloud. Turns out that the young Napoletana always addressed her mother-in-law as "Donna." She was the kindest of the four, and was there for her mother-in-law in the Donna's dotage.

While the Italians of Bensonhurst were nowhere near monolithic, neither were the Jews. From an early age I knew of Syrian and Sephardic Jews, the latter from the Iberian diaspora. I went to high school with Jaime Cassorla, a Sephardim who still spoke some of the ladino dialect of his forebears. His family's lower Manhattan apartment was hard by a Kosher pizza place. Jaime informed our Fiftieth High School Reunion class that he had become a rabbi, somewhere in the Southeast, and went by Haim (or Chaim) Cassorla (or Kassorla). Most Bensonhurst Jews were not Sephardic, but Ashkenazi, from Central/Eastern Europe, but even here there were distinctions. We Italians knew of the Litvak-Galitziana divide. We understood the differences by making parallels to the Napoletano-Siciliano fracture line. Litvaks were from up around Lithuania, and the Galitziana hailed from Galicia—no, not from Galicia, Spain, nor from Wales—but a region of Eastern Europe encompassing parts of present-day Poland (home of the bialy) and Ukraine.

Fast-forward to the Bensonhurst of today: Pauline, one of Mom's home hospice people, is a very sharp and with-it Jamaican gal. She is one of about eight kids, all doing quite well, thank you. Mom taught Pauline how to make robbies. And while this may seem culturally incongruous, how different are robbies from southern collards, or the *couve* greens that Afro-Brazilians serve with *feijoada*? About two weeks before Mom's passing, on our way to Georgette's—where we had a wonderful afternoon—we dropped in on the Mondial Bakery and pasticceria, the 20th Avenue citadel. They had a special on focaccia, and Pauline was hooked. Up to and through the last day of Mom's life, Pauline showed her true mettle, and her Jamaican "sister," Leslie, stayed up with Mom all that last night, reading to her. I still feel guilty about sleeping on the fold-out bed next door. Mom passed early the next afternoon, and I was there.

Up until at least 2013, there were three "flavors" of Sunday mass at St. Dominic's, two blocks up 20th Avenue from Mondial—Italian, Spanish, and English. At the time of Mom's passing, these were respectively presided over by an Italian, a Colombian, and a Nigerian—each very popular with the parishioners. I heard the Nigerian excoriate his church for the child abuse scandals and their cover-up. Of course, after the Italian mass, the *lingua franca* is Italian at the pastry shop. But, there could be Mexicans, Russians, Chinese, Egyptians, et al. waiting for service. "Mrs. Mondial" was serving a Mexican patron in front of me and, as they would say in Missouri, *speakin' purty darned good Spanish*. So, upon my turn, I ask, "*Y, dónde aprendiste hablar español?*" (And where did you learn to speak Spanish?) She responded, in her Sicilian accent, "On the television." Carmela, her real name, would always ask about Mom; she lost her own mother at a young age. At Mondial, I saw a Mexican guy get angry at an oblivious Chinese man for stepping in front. And I'm thinking, "Don't they know this is Italian turf?" Yea *right* Joe; just ask the Irish, and the English and the Dutch and the Native Americans before them.

At the time of her passing, Vina's building was over eighty percent Chinese—cordial and hard-working, but not the most gregarious people. Language *had* to be an impediment. You don't say, "Hey, guaglione, che se dice" to a guy who lived through the Cultural Revolution, and spoke English only so-so. Then again, this was Brooklyn, so why not? Mom had a real crisis situation with the family upstairs, whose bathroom was leaking on hers and causing water damage. This situation was amicably and equitably remedied, and sonuvagun, the family's relatives bought Mom's apartment—at a price that was very fair to us, and was made up of Chinese "lucky numbers." A Chinese-born colleague at the University of Missouri told me that there are regional differences in China in what constitutes "lucky numbers." Then again, before New York State took over gambling activities, we Italians were always looking for daily lucky numbers to play. Bookies took the bets, and couriers "ran the numbers" to the "bank." The winning three-digit number was no secret; I knew that it once was the last three of the daily double payout at a given area racetrack.

Mom missed the spontaneity of the old days, but Victor was a "throw-back." Victor was a young man in the building, with no Chinese accent (Okay, Brooklynese), and was unusual in that he had long hair and tattoos, and he always greeted Vina with a kiss. So, Aunt Vina had at least one Chinese nephew. Victor was an Italianized Chinese man, even to his first name. (Sorry folks of the court of the Khan Dynasty—we thank you very much for the polish (polacco?) you put on Marco Polo. Pasta? We had it long before Marco dropped in.) Near the end, I escorted Mom to an imaging facility in our neighborhood, for a head scan. Victor worked there. He was also going to night school. Happy to see Mom he was, but it appeared he was also dismayed that she was there. He told her he would get her taken care of right away, and was so happy to present her results, which showed little or no pathogenesis. During the first few months after Mom's passing, Sandy would come by periodically to pick up Mom's errant mail. She came across Victor on one trip. He asked about the location of Mom's grave so he could visit it. This chokes me up just writing about it.

Mom thought Victor's parents were disappointed in him. I loved that I could interact with a Chinese "brother." He emanated the vibes. Victor, man, where are you? I wish we could communicate now. Speaking of communication: Mom lived in a condo, and the monthly meetings in the downstairs lobby were a stitch. Konstantin, a thickly built Russian, was the "super" (Okay, Condo Association President, I believe), and he ran the meetings in his gravelly style. Patient he was. The Chinese had an interpreter, and some of the

Chinese oral versions had to be ten times longer than Konstantin's original. It was weird being a stand-in for Vina from B8, but I happened to be around for a couple of consecutive meetings. Mom's neighbors showed sympathy for her condition.

Inside gruff Konstantin was a Russian doll. He later persevered in the sale of B8, putting up with complex bureaucracy and escalating petty personality conflicts, because my mother was a "special person." She *was* well-liked. As was her wont, she made the artificial floral arrangements in the lobby. And, she reached out in other ways: A few years back, I had bought a subscription to *Natural History* magazine for Vina D'Agostino. When finished with an issue, Mom would leave it off for a young man in the building—kid reminded her of my son Joseph. Kid eventually went to Stuyvesant High School, and so his family and Mom had a special connection.

Many of the Italian fish markets became Chinese-owned. Often the name did not change—good to keep the old clientele, along with the new. The variety only increased, though I will never get used to seeing freshwater turtles for food, as opposed to pets. Then again, I now find the Barese favorite, *seppia* (cuttlefish).

The neighborhood changes, but as Yogi would say, "It's more of the same, even if it didn't change." And, the choices you make can drive you toward, rather than away from, "your people." Having spent some time away from the Campus Barbershop, Wayne and Travis presiding, in Columbia, Missouri, I needed a haircut. There are two "barbershops" on 20th Avenue—one a fancy Russian unisex spot, with hairdressers and a *mui gavarim pa-ruuski* sign in front. Way too fancy. Up the street, just across from St. Dominic's, which has a special shrine to Padre Pio, is Angelo's barbershop—three chairs, one barber, and he's Angelo. The place is like my stepfather's store, three decades earlier—large wood-framed glass panes on one side of a recessed wood-framed door, and no attempt at glitz or remodeling. Yes, Angelo is very functional. Except, he has a TV that transmits *only* Rai Uno, the major Italian station (I think then owned by Silvio Berlusconi). So, on a Friday evening, I pop my head in and ask if he's open on Saturday, to which he nods a "yes." The next day, I walk in, a young guy is in the chair and two older guys

Joseph C. Polacco

are in the "audience" seats. (Think of the barbershop in John Landis's 1988 film *Coming to America* with Eddie Murphy, except that nobody is African-American.) There is an Italian cartoon show on Rai Uno that no one is watching. One of the spectators is chatting with Angelo in Italian, and the other guy is reading the *New York Times*, in English of course. The young guy is finished, pays, and chats with Angelo, in Italian. The other Italian-speaker gets in the chair, and the *New York Times* guy, from his audience seat, starts to chat with Angelo, in Italian. *Mannaggia, Joe! Do you have to speak Italian to get a haircut here?*

Okay, Mr. *New York Times* is finished. My turn, and I sit in the chair, and say, *"Non parlo niente d'italiano"* (I don't speak any Italian), at which Mr. *New York Times* and a new patron laugh. Angelo, sonuvagun, refused to speak anything *but* Italian. Somehow I got across that I wanted a "buzz," with the *"macchina"* set at *"numero due, sopra tutta la testa."* I couldn't wait to get back to Mom's apartment to relay the story. When I left for the barber, Vina was alone in B8. On my return, Sandy, Toni, her husband Vinny, and Uncle Gregory's Jackie and Connie were there, visiting. Vina loved the company, and I am sure that it kept her alive.

Before I get off the neighborhood, and the touchy-feely stories, the reader might be thinking: *"Isn't this the Bensonhurst where young black Yusuf Hawkins was killed by a bunch of white kids in 1989?"* This is also the site of an ensuing march, organized by Al Sharpton; and it was far from a civil event. Yes, indeed, Bensonhurst is part of Brooklyn, the Brooklyn of the bad old Bed-Stuy and large Caribbean communities. The old days had problems, and if there were turf wars among, and within, immigrant white communities, there was worse friction between whites and people of color. New Utrecht became much blacker, as did Lafayette and Boys High. On the other side of the West End El from Marie D'Agostino sit the Marlboro Apartments, which were featured in *The French Connection.* And nestled against the opposite side of Marie's house is a new three-story "luxury condominium," the other extreme. In this checkerboard of ethnicities, races, and economic class there will be flare-ups, but I believe that the press loves to play them up, just as they romanticized mob activities. Emotions do rise, and tempers flare. But, we are all Brooklynites, and we understand each other, especially when we meet outside New York City.

During the Hawkins-inspired march through Bensonhurst, Vina went up to an African-American woman. She handed the woman a button, and said, "Peace." The lady responded with, "F___ peace, I want war." The button ended up on the ground, stepped on. I am sure that lady was a fine woman, one moved enough to go into Bensonhurst and do the right thing—march for a cause. And, I am sure that she probably regretted some things that were uttered that night, many of them directed *at* her.

But, Brooklyn is not an isolated island.

So, the oft-conflictive relations among and within the Irish, Italian, Russian, Latino are now taken up another octave to "white-black" situations. The Italian word for eggplant is *melenzana*, which in dialect sounds like *moolin-YAHNa*. The name of this lovely purple-black fruit, sometimes shortened to *moolie*, was given to black folks. This was part of Brooklynite Eddie Murphy's stand-up shtick. When we lived in back of our store, our bathroom was *the* bathroom for customers, salesmen, delivery guys, etcetera. They had to walk through our kitchen/dining room to get to it. Once, Mom was going to use the bathroom, and my grandmother Nunziatina was sitting at the kitchen table and told her in dialect, "Don't go in, there's a melenzana in there." He leaves, and tells both, "You can use the bathroom now—the moolin-yana is out."

I have not mentioned the Italian "social clubs" (*Societá di mutuo soccorso*—mutual aid societies), each anchored to a paese in the old country: Societá di Licodia Eubea, Societá Figli di Ragusa, Societá Santa Fortunata, and several others, including those connected to Belmonte Mezzagno and Sciacca, and these just in Bensonhurst or nearby. Most, if not all are now organized into the Federation of Italian-American Organizations of Brooklyn. The club sites are usually non-descript and 100% male, and the interiors feature an espresso machine, tables and a small bar, flags, and pictures of the old country. Members almost always sit out front when the weather is good. The first time I visited Napoli, I saw these very same clubs. A little girl was entreating her father to come home, because momma had dinner ready. I was back in the 'hood.

Okay, in the 'hood, Mom and I go by a club—front door's open, so we look inside (who can resist?), and there is an ebony black guy, sipping an espresso and chatting with his paisani. Turns out he is a boxer from the old country, of African extraction, but he grew up in Italy, and so he's "one of us." Links to colonial adventures in Somalia, Ethiopia, Eritrea, and Africa in general cannot be expunged: A star of Gli Azzurri (the Italian national soccer team) is Mario Balotelli, black as a melenzana, born in Palermo of African parents and adopted by a Sicilian couple.

Mom thought that black boxer hilarious; but I never heard her being openly racist. I recall her lamenting a pregnant black woman who stood up for hours ironing, as a domestic, at a friend's house. She brought street people in for a hot meal, gaining for our back-of-store home the sobriquet, "Brooklyn Rescue Mission." Michael used the name for his first CD. It featured "Willie Lo," a haunting lovely song written and sung by Bro'. It describes a poor street "bum," a black man who died of exposure in a snowstorm. Willie received some of Vina's love and charity. My brother, in his dealings with the music business, brought black colleagues to the house on several occasions. One Sunday, over the Christmas holiday, an African-American drummer and his Italian girlfriend visited us upstairs. Stepdad was "cool," and the whole visit was pleasant. When they left, Mom said: "She's pregnant." I think the couple had just found out; Mom could be a witch at times, but a good witch.

Mom developed maternal feelings for one of Michael's music buddies— Bruce J. Bruce's dad was somehow associated with the original Ink Spots. I always wondered how Bruce wound up in the 'hood, but in any case, he and Michael really bonded. Michael recently explained that Bruce was from that black enclave on the southern end of 18th Avenue, near Gravesend Bay, and that he, a Catholic, lived upstairs from the Baptist Church. The last time I saw Bruce was at Nathan's in Coney Island, on the day I flew from LaGuardia to start my PhD program at Duke. (Now, Durham—*there* was a racially interesting town.) After a gig in Manhattan, Bruce took Michael to visit his kin in Harlem. A very young child looked at Michael with horror, and cried hysterically. Bruce said something like "How does it feel to be the 'other?'"

A convalescent resident of Holy Family, a woman from the islands (Jamaica, Haiti, Bahamas, etcetera), became one of Mom's dearest friends. Most of the permanent/paid staff at Holy Family was from the islands, and so an interned *patient* from that area was fairly unique. After several messages on Mom's landline, I had to call and tell her the news of Mom's passing. The point is that in spite of sensationalistic press, black-Italian relations were often okay, and even comfortable. I can recount other vignettes, but the reader might think that I "doth protest too much," trying to paint over stark racism.

While writing this chapter, I reconnected with old friend Peter LaMontia—my best buddy from the neighborhood. Two rag-tag Italian kids, we shared passions for baseball, bugs, and football. Then we went to different high schools—Petie Thumbs to Lafayette, and I to Stuyvesant—and eventually lost contact. After fifty-five years, he popped up in my email inbox. He reminded me that black-white relations in the old neighborhood were often, well, both black and white.

> I must tell you that I adored your mother. She treated me like a son, as did all my other close friends' mothers from high school: Joe Costa's mother Irma—a great lady, who still lives on Bay 37th Street, and is close to ninety-seven years old—as well as the mothers of my friends Dom Cimino, Johnny Petrocelli, Frank Cianciosi, Steve Finn, et al. To this day we are still close. We have get-togethers every few months.

[The get-togethers make me very jealous; the stuff of novels. I need to expand on two names—Finn is short for Finnelli, and Petrocelli is the first cousin of long-time Bosox SS/third baseman, Rico Petrocelli, who played at Sheepshead Bay High School.]

I laughed when you wrote that my mother called you a pagan because you hadn't gone [to a Sunday mass]. She was a loving, protective mother who, at times, could be overly critical. I remember one time I brought home two of my buddies from 84th Street, whose parents were apartment [house] superintendents. When she saw they were black (Ronnie and Walter), she said nothing and treated them kindly, but told me afterwards never to bring them back to the house again. When I protested, she said she did not want black people in our house, case closed! As you know, racism and prejudice ran rampant in Bensonhurst—in all of Brooklyn.

I hasten to add that Mrs. LaMontia always made me feel like Petie's brother, and that my mom may have harbored the same feelings about our black friends, but she was certainly less strident, and was tempered by the diverse commerce that spilled over from the store to our home in the back. And, to his credit, my stepfather did not put his foot down either. Now, if I had come home with a black girl—that would have been different. I was pushing the color line, and got some push-back, when I stepped out with a Dominican girl a few times in high school. Ironically, the Dominicana was almost family. She was the niece of dear friend Elizabeth A., our dinner guest virtually every Thursday pasta night. "Oh, *Bainah!! I luv* your macaronis!" And she did, and we loved having her, and her more recently arrived brother's family, at our humble home. Comically, Elizabeth pronounced Vina like the Spanish *vaina*, a word for life's everyday hassles and complications. Soon after high school I gave up believing that my destiny was to marry an Italian girl. Greeks continue to amaze me for their ability to marry within "the faith," but who knows if they have undercurrents of Macedonian, Athenian and Spartan squabbles?

The twains meet; at the University of Missouri (MU) I was involved with initiatives to increase participation of under-represented minorities in the sciences. I worked with a Professor from Long Island University-Brooklyn (LIU), Dr. Anthony DePass, originally from Jamaica, and an Italian-American professor from Brooklyn's Medgar Evers College (MEC). LIU is at Flatbush and DeKalb Avenues, just off the West End DeKalb Avenue stop. Its building used to house the Paramount Theatre, site of rock and roll shows in the old days, and where Vina enjoyed Louis Prima in the even older days. The theatre stage is now a basketball court, and the lobby, with its ticket windows, is lovingly preserved. The upper floors are now offices, classrooms, and laboratories. When I was in high school, this was a *bad* neighborhood. It sure has changed, and for the better. MEC is at 1720 Bedford Avenue. Ebbets Field was at 1650 Bedford Avenue; how Brooklyn is *that*?

Back to Vina: There were MU exchange visits and joint training programs with LIU Brooklyn/MEC. Among the several students who passed through our halls was a gregarious and hardworking Puerto Rican lady from MEC. After a summer in my lab, she visited Mom upon her return to Brooklyn. Mom was nervous: "What should I serve her?" She made a rice dish, which I'm sure was out of this world, but, "Ma, *magari*, give the gal a bowl of pasta!"

The twains keep meeting, and I keep on thinking of that Missourian, Mark Twain, when I say that. Mr. Twain (Samuel L. Clemens) fully understood the evils of slavery and racism. And, Ferguson, Missouri is just down the road from me, and between Ferguson and Bensonhurst you can pick a trail with stops in Cleveland, Baltimore, Philadelphia, and Staten Island, among other places. These places, and the racially charged events that occurred in each, have taught us that we still have a way to go. And, as I finish this piece, it has become all too evident that Columbia, Missouri, and its beloved university, should be a stop on this above-ground railroad. MU made Mr. Clemens the first member of its Phi Beta Kappa Society chapter in 1901, but waited until 1950 to admit its first black student. "Concerned Students 1950" protested campus racism in 2015, leading, among other consequences, to the resignation of the statewide University System president. We are still dealing with the aftermath. Twain rhymes with pain, and almost with Lloyd Gaines, an African-American student who gained entry to the MU Law School, despite its protests. The U.S. Supreme Court ruled against MU. Gaines disappeared in 1939 before reporting for class. His whereabouts are still unknown.

Back, yet again, to Brooklyn: If it has been the uniquely fissile mixture that some might think, it has been remarkably peaceful and prosperous.

One of several Italian social clubs of Bensonhurst
Santa Maria Mutual Aid Society of Sciacca, Sicily.
Note that we still celebrate Italy's 2006 World Cup victory.

Societá del Soccorso Mutuo of Licodia, on 86th Street and 23rd Avenue.
Note the ubiquitous graffiti (Italian word, so thassa alright).
The business with the Chinese ideographs is a nail and hair salon.

The housing "Rush-in." These apartments are obviously for Russians only, or definitely cater to Russian clientele. They offer studios and one, two, or three bedrooms. My one year of college Russian always came in handy in the 'hood.

Joseph C. Polacco

16. Grandkids and Other Family

Okay, okay, Mom was a great mother to my brother Michael and to me, and to everyone else she touched, inside the family and out, in Brooklyn and beyond. So, what about her grandchildren? Quoting from a Myron Cohen skit, "Oy, don't *ask!*" Yes, she was deliriously happy to have grandkids, duhhhhhh.

The only grandchildren I bestowed upon 'Noni,' as Vina was called by them, were the children from my first marriage to Mary Schaeffer—Laura, Joseph, and Benjamin. The birth of the first two necessitated Mom traveling to foreign turf: Cali, Colombia and Durham, North Carolina. Each presented cultural and linguistic challenges. In North Carolina Mary and I were living in a humble duplex—the monthly rent was sixty-five bucks: two graduate students, now two new parents. Durham, 1966-1971, was not the college town now evoked by Coach K and his Duke Blue Devils in yet another Final Four, and by those oh-so-cute cheerleaders and the madness of the Cameron Crazies, or by Duke's gothic architecture. The campus sprang up in the 1930s, financed with tobacco money, and built, in part, by 200 imported Italian stone masons—don't start feeling superior, you Tar Heels. The Durham of my graduate studies was more of a Southern textile mill and tobacco town—definitely the place for cheap towels and tax-free cigarettes.

There was a large black section—Haiti (pronounced "Hay-Tie") or Hay-town. It had the largest black-owned business in the U.S. at the time: North Carolina Mutual Life Insurance Company. While still single, I had a redneck landlord—real character, but a product of his upbringing. He called their building, the tallest in town, "A monument to damned n___rs."

So, the Durham that Mom visited had a hard, gritty edge; there were many poor white and black folks, and even the student hangouts seemed perilous. It was a town where Gulden's Golden Mustard was found in the gourmet section of Piggly Wiggly or Winn-Dixie. Bread? Fahgeddaboudit. Mom, in the bread aisle, squeezed loaf after loaf, and exclaimed, "They're all *sponges!*"

On my first day in Durham I called Mom collect, asking to speak with "Joe D'Agostino." This was code for my having arrived in one piece. Mom was supposed to say, "Joe's not here at the moment." But, before getting her response, I had to go through the local operator—difficult: "*Suh*, I cain't understayand you!" She compounded my guilt at scamming Ma Bell to connect with Ma Vina. The phone booth felt like a confessional.

I am perhaps painting a way too negative picture of Durham. It softened, and so did I. I slowly learned how to make small talk at a slow pace, and I developed a discerning taste for barbecue and hushpuppies. I found a home in the Duke Rugby Club, and in Duke's *excellent* Biochemistry Department. And, summer graduate student softball was a blast. My advisor, Samson R. Gross, was even from Bensonhurst, fercryinoutloud. Through his lab personnel, I developed meaningful friendships in the black community. Remember, my time in Durham covered the issues of Vietnam, the draft, urban riots, such as Harlem and Detroit, student shootings in Kent State and Orangeburg, South Carolina, the assassinations of Martin Luther King, Jr. and Bobby Kennedy, and more. I even got sucked into African-American neighborhood voter registration, co-mentoring a black adolescent and, of course, protesting Vietnam on Armed Forces Day at Fort Bragg.

So, into all this comes Ma Vina from Bensonhurst, January 1970. It's a rare snowy day. The plane lands in Raleigh-Durham, and slides off the runway. Everybody is fine, and a shuttle bus has to transfer passengers to the terminal. Pilot explained the slide, and Mom exclaims, "Well, he needed snow tires!" The guy next to her almost had a conniption. At the baggage claim, Mom gives a sweet hello to a young black lady, who acknowledges it. ("Joseph, she was making a sign of the cross when the plane was sliding, and I asked her if she was scared.")

Mom sees baby Laura. She's absolutely nuts; this is her "love divine." Mom's passing was extremely hard on Laura, now a lovely lady in her mid-forties, the same age when Mom became a Noni. We had a squirrel monkey that we rescued from two disinterested undergrads. The monkey was definitely jealous of Laura, and he always greeted Mom with a squeal, a fake smile, and articulating ears. I can move my ears too, but not as well; the monkey and I share the name Carmine. Okay, Simian Carmine eventually finds a new home. But Mom, who believes in the malocchio, also believed that if Laura's mom was bitten by Carmine (the younger) while she was pregnant—a one-hundred percent air-tight happenstance—that Laura would have ear tops that flapped out at right angles to her head. She pointed this out to me. I think that the cornetto not only wards off the malocchio, but monkey ears as well.

Seafood, hmmm. North Carolina has great fishing, but the culture then was mostly fish fries, and the good marine fare did not make it that far inland to the Piedmont. Mom and I visit my favorite fish shop—the proprietor always reminded me of another North Carolinian, Barney Fife, Deputy Sheriff of Mayberry. (Don Knotts was born in West Virginia—close enough.) Barney the fish guy has a pet scarlet macaw, and the bird is raucous, and Barney constantly says, "Hush, John!" (Mom parroted this, perfecting the accent, the rest of her visit with us.) Okay, enough socializing; we want some dago fish fare. Sorry, not much, but Barney had frozen eight-inch cubes of calamari that he sold as *bait*. It was cheaper than night crawlers, and *excellent. So*, we had calamari. We invited a couple over, an Afro-Cuban and a Jewish-Italian, Jorge and Arlene—she from the Bronx and Jorge from Cuba, by way of Jersey. Mom served pasta fazool and the calamari. We could have taken Jorge out to the *paredón* (the "big wall," or firing squad—very much in use in Castro's revolution), and he would have died a happy man.

While in North Carolina, Vina managed to charm the locals—hey, they may talk slow, but they ain't stupid. She also found that the South was not a food wasteland after all—any culture that eats lots of beans and greens, well, that is Southern Italy in the Southern U.S.A.

Our son, Joseph, next in line, was born in Cali, Colombia. His crazy parents, Mary and Joseph, decided to be assistant profs at the Universidad del Valle, instead of doing the standard post-doctoral training. Hey, it *was* the Age of Aquarius, and well before Pablo Escobar. Joseph was not born in a straw hut, but in the well-equipped and well-staffed University Hospital. He was delivered by the head of Ob/Gyn, and the total cost of the hospital stay was a bottle of good scotch for the good doctor, and fifty pesos (two bucks) for a lunch in Mary's room with our new son, Joseph. The hospital staff kept on peering in to see the *gringuito* baby. He *was* cute.

So, where is *my* mom? What a trooper. She flew from JFK to Bogotá, and then transferred to a Cali flight, all by her lonesome, using English, Italian, and hand language. At the Cali airport, we were separated from Mom by transparent plexiglass until she got through all the bureaucratic rigamarole. Mom was behind the glass, chattering about all the wonders she had seen, and Mary, Joseph's mom, was looking at her and crying.

Ma Vina *loved* Cali, and the bread was much better than Durham's. She made sure we had a good *niñera*, or built-in nanny. It goes without saying that Mom fell in love with dark-eyed, olive-skinned Joseph—our nanny said he got that color 'cause he was born in Colombia. And once again, Mom had access to her "love divine, Laura." It was very tough for her to leave.

Our university colleagues really took to Doña Vina. It was amazing how they could communicate in Spanitaliano. We three, Joseph's parents and grandmother, Abuelita Vina, were feted at a place on the Rio Cali, *Aqui es Miguel*, where resident musicians serenade, for a fee, and where one can arrange for *servicio a domicilio* (home delivery), as in, "My wife is really angry at me, can you sing her favorite love songs at 3:00 a.m. outside our bedroom window?" This was so "gavoonish," Mom was completely charmed and, in turn, she charmed my Colombian colleagues. Of course, the charm of the serenade custom wore a little thin when a lady in the neighborhood, two doors away from us, was serenaded at three a.m. and little baby Joseph was awakened.

Cali was an interesting town, capital of the southwest Department of Valle del Cauca. It was nestled between two ranges of the Andes, at the base of the thick, green and wild Farallones. A group of medical students on expedition was lost there during our stay, and the rescue squad got lost as well, but they did find a plane (Bolivian, I believe) that had gone down during WWII. Eventually, the students and the rescuers independently made it out. So, it was lovely and tropical, and never really got overbearingly hot. *And*, I could play baseball on the Univalle club team. Ma Vina finally got to see me play baseball.

Although baseball was a great nexus between two worlds, baseball was also yet another reminder of the Colombian reality. When I dropped Mom off at the Cali airport for her return flight to JFK, I was wearing my baseball uniform since we had a Sunday game soon after. On the way back to town *"Miguelitos"* on the road gave me a flat tire. These charming little Mickies are tetrahedral pointed spikes in which a vertical spike always rests on a stable tripod— think of them as diabolical "jacks," and I learned much later that the history of warfare gives them to us as "caltrops," based on plant burrs/thistles by long etymology.

So someone was broadcasting caltrops to protest something; someone was *always* protesting. I arrived late at the game, which we forfeited. Thanks, Miguelitos. I mention this more as commentary than complaint, and the situation could have been much worse what with the ambushes, robberies, kidnappings and bombings that came later. We were well out of Colombia during those later troubling times of the cartels and political violence. But, the Cali of 1972-73 was never neutral—I experienced feelings ranging from exasperation/hopelessness to the excitement of learning a new vivacious culture with its own history and customs—interweaving the indigenous, African and European.

Sundays our family loved to visit a gelato place on the tony Sexta Avenida. There, a Northern Italian family sold gelato, spumoni, ices, juices and coffee. Their place was a celestial combination of tropical fruit and *gelateria*. I knew about *maracuyá* (passion fruit), *tamarindo* (tamarind), and *guayava* (guava) well before they made it to mainstream U.S.A. Okay, so we take Mom to get a gelato. We enter, and there is a short campesino-looking type at the counter, his back to Vina. She goes up to the counter, and immediately starts gabbing in a mezzogiorno dialect. I'm thinking, *Ma, what are you doing? This is Cali, not Calabria!* The patron turns towards Doña Vina, and answers in perfect dialect. How the heck did she know?

Even non-Italian speakers appreciated Mom's linguistic talents. One evening, while scouting out a place to eat, we came across a Chinese restaurant: *El Shanghai*. The place looked, well, like it was "rode hard and put away wet." Mom remarked, "Looks more like *sciangada* (shon-GAH-dah) than Shanghai." A short explanation made our caleño hosts chuckle, and I extend that explanation to you, dear forbearing reader: *Sciangada* is Neapolitan dialect for "broke-ass" or run-down. Mom and I used this word all the time, for places, things, and people.

Although Pablo Escobar was not yet a factor, other reminders that we were in Colombia were strong mafias controlling emeralds and marijuana, abundant signs of poverty, and violence as a part of the political process. Indeed, political violence during a bloody period was called "La Violencia" and its excesses led to an arrangement whereby the two leading parties, Conservative and Liberal, alternated national leadership in four 4-year terms, 1958-1974. We were in Cali during the last term 1971-1974, and the election of 1973 was tense, with military stationed at polling places. We were under lock-down the whole of election-day Sunday. While Colombia

Joseph C. Polacco

has avoided a military takeover since 1974, struggles against the FARC and ELN guerrilla movements have resulted in frequent "states of siege" placing the country under "martial law," and this has included the Universidad del Valle. Students found guilty by military tribunals were banned from the university and from much of the job market. Our family of four did not live in a vacuum. Mary and I had feet in "Two Worlds"—we interacted on a personal level with university faculty colleagues and with our own students and their families. I was a baseball teammate to University students, but also a target of protest by the very politicized student body.

We stayed only two years in Cali, and Mom was overjoyed to have us back, and close to home—nine months in Long Island (Brookhaven Labs), and then five years in Connecticut (Yale and the Connecticut Agricultural Experiment Station, in New Haven). Benjamin was born on Long Island a week before we left for Connecticut. When Benjamin was five, we moved to Columbia, Missouri. This was the nest the kids eventually left for college.

The kids' mom, Mary Schaeffer, organized a float trip: Missouri lingo for canoeing on one of our beautiful rivers in the southern half of the state. I believe we were on the Big Piney, well south of Rolla. The rest of the family—Mary, Laura, Joseph, Benjamin, and Benjamin's wife Tess—made it a two-day trip, but I took Noni back to Columbia at the end of the first day. No hard campground for my mom, though I am sure she would have loved the adventure.

The whole scene was a stitch; imagine Bensonhurst in the midst of *Deliverance* (John Boorman, Director, 1972). But, the local folks seemed to take to citified Vina. My two older kids, "Love" and "Heart Divine" did not make it too easy for their Noni. Laura and Joseph, as a result of their hijinks, lost their canoe, and had to run along the river, their canoe just floating along without them. Downstream, Mom and I observed the passing canoe, empty except for a pair of sneakers, life jackets, etcetera. It was all I could do to assure Mom that nothing was amiss, while keeping a calm façade. They finally show up; we continue.

At a turn in the river, I lost a paddle. I could see it snagged in a downed tree, but would have to leave the canoe, and Mom, to retrieve it. No way; so I awaited Benjamin and Tess, but they had stopped to fish just upstream, out of sight and beyond earshot. *Finally*, Benjamin shows up, retrieves the oar, and we continue. But, further downstream I, navigator Joe the elder, manage to capsize the canoe, in about three feet of water. Mom is completely soaked, and yells at me, "Joseph, save yourself!" Man, did I feel like a heel.

So, after a day of high adventure, Mom and I head back up north to Columbia, taking back roads. It's dark and drizzling, and I want to get home, and I am pushing it. I see a light in my rear-view mirror. A local policeman, nice young man, sees my University of Missouri ID, which I *accidently* pull out when looking for my driver's license. He shines his light on Mom's angelic face. "Okay Professor, I noticed that a tail light was out. Please get it taken care of in Columbia."

I peel out, relieved, and it seems that within a minute or two, in the burg of Vienna, Missouri, another officer pulls me over. As I tell him that I know about the tail light, he informs me that I was doing over fifty in a thirty-five MPH zone. I don't get off this time. I told him, really, that in all my years of living in Missouri—twenty years at the time—I was cited only twice for speeding, and both times with my mom in the car. (True, but I have no idea why I brought it up.) The middle-aged guy shines his flashlight on Mom—she is as stoical and placid as a Madonna—and says, "She's a bad influence on you." My experience in Vienna, when I showed up a couple of months later to face justice, is the stuff of a Hitchcockian short story. Luckily, Mom was not with me, though she would have woven the experience into a "stand-up" routine, complete with accents and colloquialisms.

Mom did two float trips with us, and I may have conflated events from them, but both floats were full of experiences that would be hard to relate to the denizens of Bensonhurst. "Ma Vina, tu sei pazza!" ("But Vina, you are *crazy!*")

Mom made float trips, attended high school and college graduations, entertained her grandkids and great-grandkids in her apartment, showed up at our Columbia home for the holidays (mainly after Stepdad passed in 1998), and was a constant in her grandkids' lives. I paraphrase Joseph: "Noni was always so peppy and funny, I thought she would live to a hundred."

During their college years, and beyond, Benjamin, Joseph, and Laura were separated from their Noni by 3,000 miles—Laura in Los Angeles, and Joseph and Benjamin in the Bay Area. But, they stayed "tight" with their Noni. Mom hated to brag about them because of the malocchio. Laura, the eldest, was Mom's "first girl," and the boys thought her title of "love divine" amusing. But there was no jealousy, as far as I could tell. Mom's love was big enough for all.

Joseph told me, when informed that I was putting "Vina" together, "Good luck, Daddy. I know Noni would be extremely moved that you are writing a book in her memory, and she would probably be just a wee bit bothered by it—the fact that you are making a fuss over her—because she was so selfless." Well, he got that right. Mom had an expression that sounded like *Quanta mossa!* It's very loosely translated as "making a mountain out of a mole hill," or "a mole hill to a mountain to a pyramid." She used this expression, for example, in reference to the modern custom of hiring a hall for catered parties for kids' first communions, eighth grade graduations, sweet sixteens, etcetera. And still, she wrote generous checks to all; and I can vouch for her tight monthly budget.

Mom was able to indulge in "girlie" stuff with Laura. She took her to see The Rockettes, the Christmas decorations and tree in Rockefeller Center, and, of course, Santa. Mom dressed Laura with her own creations—she was a living, breathing model, but with much more understated class than Barbie. They did have a special bond, and when Laura, years later, was to graduate from Berkeley (1992), Mom, Laura's mother Mary, and I flew into San Francisco International Airport. The airport limo service was going all over the Bay Area, and one of the passengers was complaining that the route could have been more direct, and that she should have been let off first. She wouldn't shut up—one of her gems: "My time is valuable; I make five hundred dollars an hour." These were 1992 dollars, mind you. Finally, she gets off, and we curious passengers are all craning to see where this talented woman lives. Mom says, "Wow, we all got stiff necks." The passengers enjoyed the commentary, and I am sure they *loved* the Bensonhurst brogue.

To save a few bucks, we three stayed at Laura's UCal co-op. The front door, of course, was always locked. Someone's (ostensible) boyfriend wanted to enter, and Noni was the only person in the lobby, and *no way* would she let him in. *Finally*, his gal comes downstairs and lets him in, and he looks at Mom, and says, "Hi, Noni." Everything was cool. At night, Noni enjoyed sharing the floor, literally, with Laura's co-op mates—she was one of the girls at a pj sleepover.

What is true at home is true everywhere—no food goes to waste. I recall a restaurant in Columbia, Missouri—Mom was in town for Benjamin's high school graduation. After dinner, we all dutifully had to stuff our pockets, bags, etcetera, with saltines, breadsticks, bread, etcetera. This was obligatory—no *way* Noni would let that food go into the garbage because of some stupid public health ordinance. And the pickles and olives at Vegas Diner, a Bensonhurst landmark—run by Greeks, of course—those were fair game also.

Joseph the younger reminisced about his Noni:

> My earliest memories are from when we all piled in the family van—the red van with the one white rear door picked up at a junkyard after being rear-ended by an uninsured driver. (My parents did their own interior 'detailing'—it was done in 2 x 4's and plywood. So, we had a floor and a back seat and very little insulation.) This was our annual holiday season trek across the frozen tundra of the Midwest and the even colder Appalachians, to a place called Brooklyn, which was like a different universe to me. After two full days and nights of car fumes, bickering, frozen tears, foggy windshields, carsickness, boredom, occasional vomiting, and what seemed like torture on wheels, we would finally make

it to Brooklyn. [Joseph, quanta mossa!!! And, we *did* lay over in a motel in Indiana. Love, Dad.] I remember ringing the doorbell of Noni and Grandpa's apartment, and having to be buzzed in—such an odd and curious thing to me—and then the long staircase leading up to the apartment. Immediately the smells of Noni's kitchen would hit me, reminding me that we had made it, and why we had undertaken such an excruciating journey.

When we got to the top of the stairs—such a vivid memory for me—Noni would grab and kiss us strongly on both cheeks over and over again; first Laura, then myself, and then Benjamin, calling us 'my love divine,' 'my heart divine,' and one more...I forget. She loved us so much, so unconditionally. Now that I look back on those early years, I realize how lucky I was to feel that kind of love, if just once a year—and I think how lucky my dad was to feel this love on a daily basis growing up as a kid. I'm sure this is why he was so crushed at her passing. Noni made me feel like someone really special and good, and here I was just an obnoxious, sheltered kid from the Midwest, not really knowing anything about the world. I wonder: If my dad didn't have such a person in his life, would he be who he is today—a bio-chemistry professor who absolutely loves what he does for a living, and someone who puts his heart into everything he does, especially raising his three kids? And would I be the same doting, loving father that I am today to my crazy little boy Luca? I'm not so sure. Luca is one lucky little boy to have a 'great-nonna' like that. And he doesn't even know it.

Much later, on one of my trips to Brooklyn, at one of Noni's Kiwanis meetings, a seven-year-old red-haired Italian-Irish boy named Vinny decided to gyrate and pump his crotch right in front of my wife Linda, and then point with both hands to his pre-pubertal genitals. Apparently this is how he thought all Asian women should be treated. It was quite funny actually, and I recounted that story to Noni on the car ride home. Noni and her friend broke into hysterical laughter—not the reaction I thought I would get from Noni. I imagined her feeling apologetic, ashamed, or angry about his behavior, but she surprised me. Noni was still young at heart—not as prudish as I thought—and we all laughed together the whole car ride home. Linda remarked once to me, 'How did your dad end up so normal growing up in a place like this?' [Elder Joe's note: What *is* normal?]

I remember a few lines from Noni that still make me laugh today...she had a way of making me laugh, and then she would join in, and then it was impossible to stop laughing. We were in her living room watching TV together—her old TV with the horrible picture. [Joseph later bought her a new TV, which is another story—again, 'Quanta mossa!'] This was when I was visiting Linda while she was at NYU. We were watching one of her favorite shows, and it goes to commercial. A Victoria's Secret commercial comes on...we both stare at it in silence for about ten to twenty seconds while half-nude models are displayed in lingerie (definitely not your iconic Noni-grandson moment). All of a sudden, Noni exclaims, 'Victoria's Secret? What's the *secret*?!' and instantly the awkward silence turns into us both rolling in laughter....

I also remember bringing up squirrels once in our conversation—I have no idea how that came up. While I'm telling my story about a squirrel, Noni interjects all of a sudden with conviction: 'Squirrels are stupid! They bury a nut, and then they can't remember where they put it!' Yes, another bout of mutually reinforcing giggling.

Mom at 2009 wedding of grandson Joseph in Tomales, California.
Left to Right: Joseph M, Laura, Mom, Joseph C., Benjamin.

Photos courtesy Polacco family

Mom content in house coat,
entertaining grandkids in the mid 1980s.

17. The West End Line

The West End is part of the BMT (Brooklyn Manhattan Transit), one of three private railroads that were subsumed into the city-run New York Transit Authority. The West End line ran a thread through my youth, like a long nerve whose ganglia were my landmarks. (Or, to really kill metaphors, like an Incan quipu rope whose knots were my gnarly episodes.) The West End was also my lullaby, even though, as Mom would say, it often had "square wheels." Transit system strikes made 86th Street eerily quiet, and sleep became difficult. When we moved upstairs, our bedrooms moved to within a first down of the tracks. Note how often the West End is mentioned in stories about Mom. The litany of stops is a rosary of experiences and memories.

What does the West End have to do with Vina? Three things:

First of all, Mom did not drive. She never even considered it, so the West End was the equivalent of Mom's taxi, especially since Stepdad only drove within a tightly circumscribed area around our store. I have no memory of him taking the subway, and most of my car rides with him were business-related: deliveries, linoleum trims, and bill collecting.

Mom and I took the El to Coney Island so I could compete in a district spelling bee. I would accompany her to downtown Brooklyn to retrieve important records, one of which later showed that she was *indeed* a year closer to Social Security age, by dint of a handwritten comment by a 1925 County of Kings (Brooklyn) census taker, which I paraphrase as: "...two sons and twenty-one-day-old girl, Vina Grandi." So, in 1987, on the eve of her sixty-second birthday, Mom was issued an updated birth certificate, and became eligible for Social Security, although at a reduced pay-out because she was born in "the notch." The West End took Mom and her two boys to both the Manhattan and Brooklyn zoos. It took us to the rodeo and the Ringling Bro's Circus, both at Madison Square Garden. This Garden was *not* on Madison Square—where its first two incarnations were located, from 1879 on. Vina, and the Garden that I knew, were both born in 1925. This third Garden remained on 8th Avenue and 49th/50th Street until 1968, my second year in grad school, the year I finally got my driver's license and bought a used, circa 1962, Pontiac Tempest she-bang.

Mom took my brother Michael and me via the El to see Santa and relatives in downtown Brooklyn. The El took Mom and my very young daughter to Rockefeller Center. Not really that many years before, Mom delivered sheep heads all over the city for her grandfather's successful Italian deli. The heads, or *i capuzelli*, were de rigueur for Easter. Mom's maternal grandfather, Nonno Giovanni Rainone, took his family of four to America, including my own Nonna Nunziatina, then a *ragazza* of fourteen. I could write a book about Nonno's misadventures, including being accused of pushing counterfeit olive oil during the WWII embargo on Italian imports, and of being a Mussolini sympathizer because he ran a U.S.–Italy Cultural Center on his store's second floor. He won those cases, but he eventually lost his store and two buildings in the long depression.

Secondly, the West End was *my* wheels. As a city kid I never even thought about owning a car. And since Mom did not drive, she *had* to trust my safety as I rode *alone* on the subway, a generic term encompassing the West End and the other many lines. As I got older, my travels were increasingly alone or, more dangerously, with my buddies. "Dangerously," because as I got older, I did not necessarily keep pace by "growing up." But, I fooled enough people; for instance, I became a courier for Bensonhurst Junior High School, and navigated the West End, and its connections, to all parts of the city. The West End took me to an entrance exam at Stuyvesant High School, at the 14th Street Manhattan stop—Union Square. I was intimidated, and convinced I would not be accepted. But, later I took the West End to attend that same school and the same West End to its graduation ceremony in Carnegie Hall. Before Lincoln Center, Carnegie Hall was a *big deal.*

My baseball teammates and I would take "the train" to games in Coney Island and the Parade Grounds, which seemed to me the Elysian Fields. I am proud to say that my parents *never* drove me to a game, be it Little League, grasshopper, Babe Ruth, high school, whatever. Helicopter parents, in the modern sense, I did *not* have. But I feel Mom ever hovering, even now.

If Mom worried about me on the West End, she worried more about bro' Michael in any conveyance or on the street. At the end of a day, and amid the streaming humanity of 86th Street, she would belt out in her strong Mezzo-Soprano: "*Michaellllll!*" No doubt this caused some inner ear problems among the shoppers and returning West End commuters.

And third, the West End Line was essential for our immigrant integration into America. In addition to the West End being Mom's taxi, and later my own transportation, it was a "vehicle" by which Mom, and her mom, learned to cope. Nonna Nunziatina was very hearing impaired, from a childhood disease incurred in Italy; so she spoke little English, despite living in America since the age of fourteen. But, she could *really* navigate the trains, and she learned how to recognize lines by the number and color of lights over the conductor on the approaching first car. Of course, daughter Vina was often my grandmother's guide, and when people were rude to Nonna (it sounded to me like a-NO-na), she would use a "play-on-words" hand signal meaning both, "How do I get there?" and, "Go f--- yourself." Nonna would then tell daughter Vina, quite audibly, "*Quest'americano non capisce niente*" (This American doesn't understand anything), but "*quest'americano*" was elided to sound like "*questa merda di cane*" (this piece of dog shit). She *was* a pistol and I can see where some of my punsterism had its roots.

A twice-told tale is Mom and Nonna taking an early train out of Brooklyn to Delancey Street to shop for haberdashery. They understood that the Jewish merchants felt they *had* to close a sale to the first customer of the day, or it would be a bad day. Nonna Nunziatina was a *hard* bargainer, and Mom, though feeling for the proprietor, helped with translation and followed orders. For instance, they would feign leaving, under Nonna's whispered instructions, "*Non guardare indietro!*" (Don't look back!), until hearing a plaintive "Signora" from the owner. They usually got back on the train with socks and underwear, and at a good price.

"The West End Line" was swallowed by the renaming mania of NYC Transit, and now is called the "D Line," not to be confused with the "D Train" of the old days. Why try to expunge the history, lore, and lure of the New York Subway system by renaming all the lines with letters and numbers? Surely, it is no easier to navigate now. However, New Yorkers persisted in calling "the D" the West End, and the name is now making a re-appearance, as if a fossil still living. Makes me think of the "living fossil fish," the coelacanth, and indeed, the New York Aquarium on Coney Island, accessible at The first West End stop, is very much involved in preserving and documenting this fish in the wild. The West End is mostly elevated in Brooklyn, and it seems to me that only 86th Street lives comfortably under its shadow. Then the tracks go, seemingly reluctantly, underground before reemerging to go over the Manhattan Bridge, where the view alone is worth the price of a subway fare, before burrowing under Manhattan to the last stop on 57th Street, close to Columbus Circle.

So, indulge me as I try to go at Express speed through the stops of the West End of my youth. I have given them numbers, though timorously, because the NYC Transit Authority might embrace the practice.

1. Coney Island

Not just the iconic resort area, but also a train junction, with connections to the three other BMT lines, including the Brighton Beach to Prospect Park. The latter station sported understated small white plaques that read, "Ebbets Field/Baseball Park." On the way, get off at Brighton Beach to visit Harvey Keitel.

Coney Island (Stillwell Avenue) station had its own concessions, and always smelled like fries, taffy, knishes, salsiccia, cuchifritos, and salt water. Mom brought her own food to the beach, of course, but she did treat us to a Nathan's frank once in a while. Cotton Candy? Ma, quando, *mai*! Music was all around, from honky-tonk to soul to Latino. One place always had a real live singing cowboy, standing on the bar right there on the Boardwalk. Coney embraced you as the car doors opened; you could easily tell out-of-towners by their reaction. And, little known to outsiders, Nathan's Famous was always open, even in the depth of winter—hot dogs, riffled fries, and clams on the half shell could be had at 2:00 a.m. in the company of fellow freezing humanity. Coney Island became baaaaad in the 60s and 70s, though two Italian restaurants, Gargiulo's and Carolina, did well, even later grabbing razed tenement space for parking. Carolina eventually passed. Nathan's survived, prospered, and begat franchises beyond Coney. A night at Gargiulo's is iconic "Godfather."

Mom arranged for Michael and me to have summer memberships, first in Ravenhall, the Italian swim club, and the next summer in Washington Baths, the Jewish one. There were city lifeguards on the beach and club guards by the pool, though the biggest danger was Ravenhall's clientele. I witnessed a real-life cop chase, with the culprit, a non-member I believe, being captured in the solarium of the dressing area—talk about feeling naked, especially in the presence of drawn guns. This guy tried to knock off a loan company on Bay Parkway, and somehow ended up in Ravenhall's maze of outdoor lockers. He passed me, sweaty in an overcoat; I was too young to expect him to flash me. But, *real* mobsters were members of Ravenhall. Outside their cabanas, they grilled steaks, drank scotch, and strutted their stuff. And you couldn't show no disrespect—ya know what I mean? There was a bunch of younger wannabees; don't make no eye contact wit dese guys. Some of bro's friends were "trouble-makers," and that often meant that big Bro'

　　　　　　　　　　　　　　　Joseph C. Polacco

(yours truly) had to stand in. Punking out of a fight was not an option, but there were beautiful ballets of posturing, strutting, and talkin' da talk. (Mike claims that I provided "muscle" to preserve his shoeshine "franchise" on the corner of 86th Street and Bay Parkway, but all I remember is showing up and looking a little crazy.)

Don't get me started on the Cyclone Roller Coaster, or the Parachute Jump. I will just mention that I saw a national ranking placing the Cyclone in the nation's top ten. Well, to me it was number one, because the structure was made of *wood*, and the attendants all looked like disinterested, senile alcoholics. That first drop—most devastating I ever experienced.

This is about Vina, but I could write a book about Coney: Grasshopper baseball at Mark Twain Junior High fields, the Tuesday nite Fireworks when the Dodgers were in Brooklyn, the washed up smelly dead whale on display—for a price, the freak shows, tackle football on the beach, the sub-culture under the boardwalk, Gypsy fortune tellers, beach rock and roll shows by DJ impresarios, Murray the K and Cousin Brucie. Vina is now on my shoulder and yelling, "Joseph, *ancora!*" (Enough already!)

Sorry, Ma, but when I left Brooklyn I began to appreciate how Coney was, and still is, ingrained in American consciousness. We had *such* material, and did not appreciate it. *Brooklyn*, the 2009 novel and the 2015 movie both feature 1953 Coney Island. Not appreciated now, was a 1953 movie, *The Little Fugitive* (Morris Engel, Ruth Orkin and Ray Abrashkin, Directors) that starred neighborhood street kid Richie Andrusco. It portrayed his escape to Coney Island after being tricked into believing he killed his brother. Michael and I both knew Richie, and stardom made him unbearable in our eyes. The point here is not to complain about that little redhead, Richie, but to alert readers that *The Little Fugitive* is a great documentary of 1953 Coney Island. The film has a home movie quality, which plays up the Carny atmosphere of Coney. It was nominated for several awards and won its directors the Silver Lion at the 1953 Venice Film Festival. And I admit, Richie was good.

2. Bay 50th Street

Sicilian turf, and the start of the three-station chase in *The French Connection*. Lots of D'Agostino lore took place at this stop, a short hop, for instance, to the Most Precious Blood Parish and its street festival. This was also the stop of John Franco—legendary lefty reliever of the Mets.

3. 25th Avenue

Now we're on 86th Street, and not far from the Spumoni Gardens (27th Avenue and 86th Street), a Brooklyn treasure since 1939. This is the site of a possibly constructed memory of my biological father Mike Polacco. He was the life of the party, holding me in his arms there, while Mom did not seem pleased.

4. Bay Parkway

My stop—where you went to sample the emporia, open-air stands, and crushing humanity of 86th Street, especially between Bay Parkway and 23rd Avenue. Not far were the spawning grounds of Barbara Streisand, Elliott Gould, and, of course, "wise guy" Henry Hill, who used to shake down the cabbies at the taxi stand under the station. Oh, ans the West End reinforced that us neighborhood kids were "outer borough": the Manhattan- and Coney Island-bound sides are, respectively, "To City," and "From City".

5. 20th Avenue

This is the stop for "Sorority of the Strong."

For neighborhood residents of my age, I mention the mysterious "bra store" somewhere around 20th Avenue on the south side of 86th Street. We *all* had to be aware of this store—was it *really* abandoned? It had the same one-piece corset-bra in the window, seemingly for years. We watched it age and senesce. Now, 86th Street was always busy, and while there was turnover of businesses, no store would appear to be deserted for years on end. Bro' Michael remembers the store, cause he wanted to buy a "large" bra for his Ma, so she could

Joseph C. Polacco

"hold her own" with some of the buxom ladies in her circles. No way he could find the store open, and had to move closer to 13th Avenue to a place that would serve and humor him.

6. 18th Avenue

This used to be oh-so-Italian, named Cristoforo Colombo Boulevard at 86th Street, just as it turned non-Italian. But 18th Avenue, closer to the waterfront, also had a small black enclave with a Baptist Church. Legend has it that Mike Tyson spent some of his youth here, but that may be apocryphal. However, this was indeed Bruce J's stop.

I don't want to get *troppo italiano* on you, dear reader, but this stop has two links to my biological roots—the *Baresi* (Bari) of Dad, Mike Polacco, and Mom's Napoletani (Naples). Bari is in Puglia, on the upper Achilles tendon of the boot, facing Albania. But the Bari Pork Store, "King of the Sausage and Salumeria," has been on 18th Avenue and 63rd Street for forty plus years. It makes its own mozzarella, ricotta, etcetera on site, and features pig carcasses hanging from hooks. If you're going to go non-Kosher, or non-Halal, go all the way. Back in Bari, a popular fare is horsemeat, and I have seen its butcher shops in Puglia. But that custom died out among the new world *Baresi*. For a few years, I had a charming memento—a calendar from the Bari Pork Store—hanging in my University of Missouri office. It was like a miniature wicker-type curtain, easily rolled up. Seemingly hand-painted iconic scenes of the old country shared the spotlight with a clearly stated, "Made in China."

Not to be outdone, Naples is well-represented by Vincent Gardenia Boulevard, at the intersection of 16th and Benson Avenues, a block south of 86th Street. Character actor, Vincent (Vincenzo) Gardenia was born in Naples, but lived in Bensonhurst virtually all his life. He appeared in movies, *Moonstruck* (Norman Jewison, Director, 1987), *Bang the Drum Slowly* (John D. Hancock, Director, 1973) and in plays including *God's Favorite*, *California Suite*, and *The Prisoner of Second Avenue*. To me, he was an Italian leprechaun.

And, the web of relations in Bensonhurst links Mom with Mr. Gardenia. She and Stepdad knew him, and thought he was a great guy. Moreover, Gardenia and his father, Gennaro Scognamillo Gardenia performed with "Farfariello," Large Mary's Uncle Eduardo (Migliaccio), in the early twentieth century Italian Theatre (described in *The Italian-American Immigrant Theatre of New York City*, by Emelise Aleandri, 1999).

7. 79th Street

Exit the station in the "To City" direction to New Utrecht High on 80th Street, or, exit in the "From City" direction to Loew's Oriental Theatre on 86th Street, which was featured in the opening scenes of *Angie*, (Martha Coolidge, Director, 1994, starring James Gandolfini and Geena Davis).

From the moving train, there is a perfect view of the field of New Utrecht High. The Utes at one time were a New York Public School grid power. New Utrecht and Lafayette, in my neighborhood and accessible from the Bay 50th Street or 25th Avenue stops, played in the Thanksgiving "Pasta Bowl." The Utes' legendary coach, Sy Rapp, though, was Jewish, and the Utrecht field honors him by bearing his name.

This is the same field seen in the credits to *Welcome Back, Kotter*. John Travolta—Vinny Barbarino—was a regular, before starring in *Saturday Night Fever* (John Badham, Director, 1977). For the latter role he obtained his wardrobe in the 86th Street and 21st Avenue men's store, *The Male Attitude*, under the El, of course. Stepdad, and his buddy Seymour Willinger, tried to update their wardrobes at the emporium. Mom said something like they were suffering from slow-motion vasectomies in those disco pants.

Lafayette, not to be outdone, and consistent with the old Bensonhurst Italian-Jewish tradition, offered legendary lefty Sandy Koufax, his teammate Fred Wilpon, the Mets majority owner, Nick Martino, middleweight Golden Glove champion and football coach Sam Rutigliano (1956-58) who was 1980 NFL Coach of the Year with the Cleveland Browns. Baseball's Joe Torre attended a Catholic high school, but lived across the street from Lafayette. Names in the 'hood too numerous to recount include Paul Sorvino, Larry King, and Jerry Della Femina. But, I carry on.

There was also the other side of celebrity, and 79th Street marked the demise of bad boy Jimmy Emma—"whacked" circa 1977 while washing his car under the El (described in *Underboss* by Peter Maas, 1997). Jimmy was too much of a loose cannon, even for the mob families, and had to go. He and I had some interactions, mostly through my brother. Thankfully, we were cool, 'cause I saw him go berserk on others, for trivial or imagined slights.

Mom knew the whole story of the hit, as did much of Bensonhurst— "Who needs a stinkin' book?" as you might hear on the street. The story included Ramper Gerard Pappa, who escaped the hit scene by jumping through the open rear window of a passing car. Gerard got his at the Villa 66 on 14th Avenue and 66th Street, some years later. This I was also told by Mom, plus other details. The story was not relayed as some epic local legend, but as a sorry comment on the low-life wise guys. She also felt very sorry for the Emma and Pappa families.

Old friend Pete Lamontia reminded me very recently about Emma's sidekick, Free-zee:

> "Well, I kinda remember him as being a not-so-tough guy. He was mean, but with a slight soft touch—a hood with a heart so to speak, an under-ling to Jimmy Emma. Free-zee was good to me only because of my athletic prowess. He would always pick me to be on his square-ball team, because of my speed. [Hoods playing square ball? Those *were* different times.] If he and his gang would see me on the street while looking for someone to beat up, they would just pass me by. The last I can recall is that he eventually ended up in jail."

The "Rampers" named themselves after the footbridge "ramp" that crossed the Belt Parkway at 17th Avenue—from Bath Beach Park to

Gravesend Bay. Sammy "The Bull," Jimmy, Gerard, et al. used to hang there by the bay. For many years, even though I had studied physics and solid geometry, I thought of a ramp as a gentle arch. My college-educated uncle, Mark Harris, reminded me that a ramp was an inclined plane, the kind that Galileo and Newton employed to develop their laws of motion.

Finally, I am bringing up memories from my hormone-addled adolescence. I passed the 79th Street stop, to and from all-male Stuyvesant High School. Probably even the more worldly dudes from Brooklyn Tech would look forlornly at the Ute gals getting on and off, and it seemed that their looks back abetted our pain—girls can be cruel.

8 and 9: 72nd and 62nd Streets

"Fly-by" stations: the train stopped, of course, but I was usually passing through, and passing them meant I was on my way to Manhattan, or back home to Bensonhurst. I used to note the differences in passengers getting on and off—definitely folks of my ethnicity compared to travelers closer to Manhattan. 74th Street and New Utrecht Avenue marked "Pastosa Ravioli," which could provide a year's sustenance to the Italian space station.

There used to be a vineyard off 62nd, I think some fazool from the old sod bought grapes and produced wine. He undoubtedly had his own vines, as did many folks in Bensonhurst—if nothing else, they made a great arbor over driveways. You can catch the Sea Beach Line at 62nd and visit my Nonna—she called the line something like "Sumnabeech," as did many other riders, in their own argot.

10 and 11: 55th and 50th Streets

Located in the heart of Hasidic Borough Park, these were the stops for Maimonides Medical Center. Mom would arrive daily at 7:00 a.m. when Stepdad was near death (1998), and leave at 7:00 p.m. back for Bay Parkway, then walk the eleven blocks to her apartment. This was also the scene of Mom's cancer struggles.

12 and 13: Fort Hamilton Parkway and 9ᵗʰ Avenue.

These were usually fly-by stations. However, 9ᵗʰ Avenue was in Sunset Park which had real symbolism in the bad old days. Bro' and I often went to the public Sunset Pool, which made Coney Island seem as mild as Disneyland. Elizabeth's refugee Dominican family lived at the 9ᵗʰ Avenue stop.

14. 36ᵗʰ Street

A "major" stop and transfer to other lines. When on my rambles in the city of Manhattan, 36ᵗʰ Street was my goal—once reached, it was a sure way to catch the West End home.

15. Pacific Street

Pacific is a "mega-station" in which you can do a "transcontinental walk" to Atlantic Avenue, now the stop for the Barclay Center, the area that was *supposed* to house the covered stadium for the Brooklyn Dodgers in the late 50s. I do not buy into revisionist history. If O'Malley really wanted that stadium, it would have happened. How could he lead Los Angeles by the nose, and *fail* to get New York and New Jersey Port Authority czar Robert Moses to agree to the stadium?

15a. DeKalb Avenue

Note, yet another Dutch name. Why stop number 15a and not 16? Because we never knew if this was the last stop in Brooklyn, and upon arriving at Pacific Street, there was the eternal question: "Does this train stop at DeKalb Avenue?" If not, you were on Canal Street, in Manhattan. The smart-ass guys at Brooklyn Tech knew, though. This was their stop. They were rivals of my high school, Stuyvesant. Somehow, Brooklyn Techies never acquired the "nerd" veneer of the Stuyvesant Peglegs.

Pieter (Petrus) Stuyvesant was the last Dutch Governor of New York (Nieuw Amsterdam before the English took over in 1644). His silver-encrusted peg leg replaced the leg he lost years earlier on the

Caribbean island of St. Martin/Sint Maarten, in a battle with the French—or was it the Spanish? I was told, while vacationing in St. Martin, that Stuyvesant gave up Nieuw Amsterdam for Surinam in South America—seemingly a good trade at the time. He coulda been the Mets' General Manager.

DeKalb was also the stop for the Brooklyn Fox Theatre, where Murray Kauffman (Murray the K) ran his rock and roll shows of the 60s and 70s. These were definitely integrated affairs, and my brother was able to get close to the business by being an errand boy. He tells a comical story of being chased by young black ladies as he carried Jackie Wilson's pants to the cleaners between shows. Surely you have heard Wilson's rendition of "Your Love" (Keeps Lifting Me) Higher and Higher (Gary Jackson, Carl Smith, 1967). Don't forget that Michael also had a running career, naturally.

16. Canal Street

The stop for Delancey Street, Chinatown, and Little Italy.

On my Nonna Nunziatina's marriage license of 1917, Nunziata Rainone and Angelo Grandi are respectively listed as living on the Little Italy streets of Mott and Broome. Though Mott Street was reputedly a Calabrian enclave, the newlyweds gave their hometown as "Naples."

Whatever their Old World origin, the Italian kids seemed to control the firecrackers coming out of Chinatown. You ventured here from Bensonhurst ready to negotiate hard and not be intimidated, and you had better come with friends.

If Vina only knew what we were up to.

Sorry, Ma.

17. 14th Street–Union Square

From 14th to 42nd Streets the West End ran along diagonal Broadway, which, when intersecting major avenues identified a Square at each a stop. Union Square used to be the setting for soap box purveyors of various political positions. I would get off here, and walk down to Stuyvesant High School of Science on 15th Street and 3rd Avenue, trying to avoid the bums in the park and the tough girls in front of Mabel Dean Bacon Vocational High School of Nursing. Actually, I believe it was an Annex. We Stuyvesant guys, and we were all guys, seemed to be mostly sexual ingénues. I recall such comments from the ladies as, "Hey boy, you kinda cute! Yea, I'm talkin' to *yoo.*"

Of course, I could have bypassed the bums and the Mable Dean Bacon (Annex) girls by transferring to the cross-town Canarsie line, getting off at 14th Street and 3rd Avenue. But, there was no honor in that.

I was in Stuyvesant during the Cold War years of 1959-1962. The air raid sirens went off one afternoon, and the professor of solid geometry, Doc Brody, ordered us to take cover under our wooden seats, 'cause no one had heard anything about a test that day. One kid behind me was whimpering.

Back to Mom: In the neighborhood, I was relatively well-accepted by my macho dago cousins and friends, though a nerd, and a little different. I think playing sports, and relatively well, saved me from a few beatin's. And, in my few fights, I handled myself with honor. But, most importantly, Mom defended my interests in spiders, bugs, snakes, chemistry set experiments, and my subscription to *Scientific American.* And, I was also respected—and let me say this with total candor—by my Jewish classmates; I even helped some with their homework. We all knew the value they put on education, and those values rubbed off on Mom.

So, where did I keep spiders, bugs, and snakes in those cramped three rooms? I didn't. I carved out my own little study/lab in the back of the store basement. All through Stuyvesant High School, I did my homework there; I will never appreciate how much Mom "skeeved" the critters, but defended my keeping them in the basement.

Linguistic detour: To skeeve is an Anglicization of *schivare,* to avoid, more likely, *schifare,* to loathe. Something you try to avoid, something repulsive, is something you "skeeve." And, a repulsive person is a *schifazzo* (ski-VOTZ). And, along the schifare vein, the West End line was indirectly responsible for frequent sewer back-ups in our basement. Its girders and the heavy traffic under the elevated tracks, and the trolleys at street level made sewer line improvements difficult, and the old system was often overwhelmed. The situation was eventually remedied, but well after I left for college. Sam "Unger the plumber" resembled the older Albert Einstein, and I still can see Sam's long-suffering expression looking up at me while he stood knee-deep in the bilge. He was not thinking of the time-space continuum. So, I did not always have access to my study.

My taking the Stuyvesant entrance exam was a natural consequence of encouragement by Mom and my teachers. I thank Miss Brady, my ninth grade social studies teacher, who informed me that I "made Stuyvesant." Without another breath, she followed with, "and, you're going." Miss Brady was Irish, but most teachers back in the day were Jewish, and I was encouraged by many. An eighth grade science teacher, after answering one of my questions, followed with a smiling, "and your question tells me that you're reading *Scientific American*." Words can hurt deeply, but can also lift you to the heavens.

Pete LaMontia, my good buddy and co-conspirator in baseball and bugs, was also instrumental in channeling me to Stuyvesant; from there, being catapulted to an out-of-town college was a natural progression, though not obvious to me at first. Mom was very excited one day at the dress shop because I was coming home for semester break. One of her cohorts asked, "From jail?"

But, I was no angel, either. How can one attend high school in Manhattan and not be tempted by its attractions? On a few occasions I gave in to playing hooky to shoot pool at iconic Julian's Billiard Academy on Union Square. No, I never rendezvoused with a Mabel Dean Bacon nursing student there—drat.

18. 23rd Street
Madison Square, but not the site of the Garden since 1925. This, to me, was a "way station." Mom was born in 1925, the year the Garden moved uptown.

19. 34th Street
Herald Square didn't mean that much to me. But, my wife Nancy *loves* Macy's on Herald Square. Gimbel's, though, is now just a memory.

For Michael, in his youth, this stop was *very* special. Michael and I shared the same bed until I went off to college—we had no room for anything else. Ours was a folding bed, in an activities room by day, bedroom by night. To get to it we went through the store, the kitchen, and our parents' bedroom, which doubled as a living room. Sharing the bed got dicey when Michael got an Olympic case of athlete's foot, or eczema, or whatever. It was painful, and he had to keep his feet bandaged with gauze and tape. Mom took him to the New York Skin and Cancer Hospital at East 38th Street in Manhattan, where the attending doc said it was the most severe case of athlete's foot he'd ever seen. (Who ever said we weren't athletic?) Michael was about eight years old, and I eleven, and the treatment duration was at least a year and a half.

He was treated first weekly, then bi-monthly. Mom turned this unpleasant experience into something special for Michael, turning each visit into their little secret West End date day. They would leave during the morning rush hour, though Michael's appointments weren't until late morning. After the appointment, they would spend the next few hours going to what became their special places in New York. It began with a simple frankfurter and orange juice at Nedick's, and advanced to trips to museums, parks, and the zoo. This was sweet, and I never felt jealousy, certainly not to the point that I wanted in on that foot condition. Michael did try to gross me out on a few occasions, though. He succeeded.

20. 42nd Street –Times Square

Anyone who has seen *Midnight Cowboy* (John Schlesinger, Director, 1969) gets a gist of the way it was. The sex shows and porno shops are now mostly gone, but that stupid cowboy in his tightie-whities is a throwback. I should have mentioned him to Mom for a poetic urban sound bite. And, Mom would prefer a month of fasting to paying the prices at a Times Square deli.

21. 47th/49th Street and 7th Avenue

I'm just an outer-borough kid, what could interest me here in the theatre district? Well, I got to see Rita Moreno and company in *West*

Side Story live at the Winter Garden at 50th and Broadway. How did a fifteen-year-old swing tickets? A few guys and I spent hard days stripping paper off the walls of a friend's apartment in Brighton Beach, just east of Coney Island. His dad was a Broadway agent, and he paid us with tickets. I could *not* believe how out-of-towners just ate up gang wars—a bane of my existence. Jimmy Emma, if you hanged on like Harvey Keitel did, you too "coulda been a contendah."

This was an exciting stop—lots of action, and the site of the Garden from which I came back very late one night. Mom was sleeping on folded arms at the kitchen table. I sneaked past, so as not to disturb her. She woke up—I don't know how many hours later—in a panic, until she saw me asleep in the bed I shared with Michael who, Ave Maria, was there also.

Noni Vina got off here, and trekked a couple of avenues over to Rockefeller Center to show granddaughter Laura the Christmas tree and the ice skaters. Radio City Music Hall's Rockettes were within shouting distance. It was definitely a "girl's day" out.

22. 57th Street and 7th Avenue

Yes, Carnegie Hall, where Harry Belafonte, another kid from another 'hood, gave a performance and sang special numbers for the folks in the scholarship section. Columbus Circle, one block west, was the site of 1970 and 1971 rallies by the Italian-American Civil Rights League. The organizer, ironically and tragically named Joe Colombo (capo of one of the five New York crime families), was shot three times in the head during the 1971 event. The movement was killed, and Joe was in a coma until he died in 1978.

Beyond 57th Street

Mom would give me a dope slap if I got too symbolic, about a rag-tag Italian kid starting off in South Brooklyn, and attending his high school graduation at Carnegie Hall—almost two extremes of the old West End line. Ahh, but indeed, my horizons expanded. North of 57th was all of Central Park, rife with memories, Harlem, Randall's Island, where Stuyvesant played home football games at Downing (now

Joseph C. Polacco

Icahn) Stadium, Columbia University, the Polo Grounds in Coogan's Bluff on the Harlem River, Yankee Stadium, and the glorious Bronx. And, then, there was Ithaca in upstate New York.

At Cornell, after a freshman year of trying to be a 165-pound offensive guard, I went out for lightweight football. We had to make weight (154 pounds), and we played *real* tackle football, on regulation fields, with footballs that were *not* deflated. The league was comprised of Cornell, Columbia, Princeton, Penn, Rutgers, Army (West Point), and the Naval Academy.

So, during my sophomore year in 1963, Cornell plays Columbia at Baker Field on West 218th Street, at the extreme northern tip of Manhattan, about 160 blocks North of Carnegie Hall. The field is now Robert K. Kraft Field at Lawrence A. Wien Stadium—obviously folks who donated a few bucks. Michael, Momma Vina, and Franca, a Sicilian immigrant gal from upstairs, go out to Baker Field. I have *no* idea how they made it up there, but according to Mom it was a trek. They may have taken a train into the Bronx, and then traversed a bridge back south.

Columbia does not draw that many fans in general, and a lightweight football game was almost a family affair. Mom's emotions alternated between excitement and absolute horror. Mom thought I either threw my body too much (I was a tackle, so I had to release downfield at times), or wound up too much at the bottom of the pile. After each play, Mom, hiding her head, raised it only long enough to moan, "Oh, no!" and "Where's Joseph?" So, during one series, my chinstrap was unbuckled. Mom asks Michael, who was playing high school football at that time, "Why is that strap hanging down from Joseph's hat? All the other boys have their hats on right." Michael assured her that I would fasten it, and I heard, in the silence before the next play, "Now boy, put your strap on!" The small crowd was definitely amused by this Vina character.

Game over; we win, and we gather 'round the team bus for the trip back to Ithaca. We are all in our Ivy suits and ties. Mom comes over with Franca. Now, she was a beautiful girl, and blessed by the goddess Venus, and my teammates *loved* her accent. "Who is she, Joe?" When

I said, "the girl upstairs," they nearly blew a collective gasket. Up there in Ivy-landia, and in suburbia, it's always "the girl *next door*." As I board the bus, Mom yells, holding a brown paper bag, "Joseph, I brought you an egg sandwich!" I yell back that we were going to be rewarded with a steak dinner on the way to Ithaca. My teammates, already energized by being in NYC, were very much amused. I recall singing, "When you're a Jet, you're a Jet all the way..." the night before, outside our hotel. Once on the bus, one of the coaches has the day's *New York Post* or *Daily News* on his lap, and the headline says: "Joe Bananas, Call Him Dead." So I say, reflexively, "Oh *no*! They got Joe Bananas." My teammates went ballistic: "Did you hear what Polacco said?" On the way back they were singing the banana boat song, when they weren't singing the praises of Franca. And Vina D'Agostino helped make this a very memorable day. Was she embarrassed? Shy? Heck *no*; she was there for her boy.

By the way: Joe "Bananas" Bonanno was *not* whacked, he was just on the lam for a couple of years (smart). He died of natural causes at ninety-seven, and his career is littered with famous mafia names.

Oh, and that egg sandwich was probably Sicilian potatoes and eggs, on good semolina bread—definitely can hold its own with most steaks.

———————————————

RIGHT: The old West End, from Coney to 57th Street.

The lines coming out of Coney Island are now the D (West End), N (Sea Beach), F (Culver) and B (Brighton Beach). The West End of my high school days in the early 60s was "co-linear" with the current D in Brooklyn, crossing over the Manhattan Bridge. Beyond the Manhattan Bridge, the West End followed what is now the N line to its last stop at 57th Street, a block East of Columbus Circle. Condensed aromas-induced hypnosis at each stop would provoke raw material for a New York novel.

The approximate location of Stuyvesant High School is marked by an "x" on the Canarsie Line going east from 14th Street–Union Square.

Joseph C. Polacco

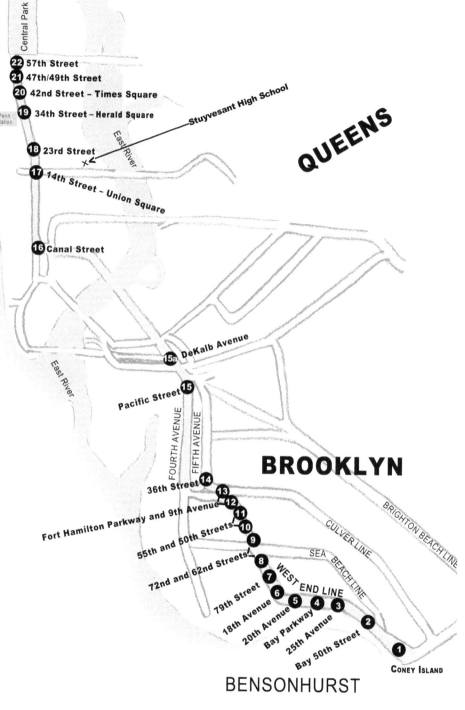

MANHATTAN

Central Park

Penn Station

22 57th Street
21 47th/49th Street
20 42nd Street – Times Square
19 34th Street – Herald Square

Stuyvesant High School

18 23rd Street

East River

17 14th Street – Union Square

16 Canal Street

QUEENS

East River

15a DeKalb Avenue

Pacific Street **15**

FOURTH AVENUE

FIFTH AVENUE

BROOKLYN

36th Street **14**
13
12
11
Fort Hamilton Parkway and 9th Avenue

55th and 50th Streets **10**
9

CULVER LINE

72nd and 62nd Streets **8**
7
79th Street **6**
18th Avenue **5**
20th Avenue **4**
Bay Parkway **3**
25th Avenue **2**
Bay 50th Street **1**

SEA BEACH LINE
WEST END LINE

BRIGHTON BEACH LINE

CONEY ISLAND

BENSONHURST

Vina

86th Street and Bay Parkway, 1940. I lived one block to the left (West), off the corner of Bay 31st Street. A "Candy Store" (and newsstand) is still there, where I helped Harry and Morty assemble gargantuan Sunday papers. Last I looked the place was run by a family from the Indian sub-continent. "Times Square" is now a Turkish restaurant, the "Istanbul." Now gone are the trolleys tracks, available parking and the Bay Parkway taxi stand, just around the corner, where Henry Hill used to shake down cabbies. The other side of the El is shown in the following photo, albeit twenty years later.

Photo, reproduced with permission, from "Brooklyn's Bensonhurst, Bath Beach, and New Utrecht Communities, a Photographic History," Brian Merlis with Lee A. Rosenzweig. Allen Kent, consultant.

Joseph C. Polacco

86th Street produce, near NE corner with Bay Parkway, 1960. This scene seems much too sane to me. Two-wheeled shopping carts are more in vogue now. Total purchases were usually summed, in saliva-moistened pencil point, on a paper bag. Three storefronts are shown, and the far right housed Schlom and Deutch bakery (2205), apparently gone by 1960. The establishments are Jewish; but note the lowest wooden box in the forefront bears the name, "DiGiorgio Fruit Corporation." Grapes are 19¢/lb—hurry.

Photo courtesy Brian Merlis.

Vina

86th Street, looking west towards 20th Avenue 1917. (21st Avenue and Bay Parkway are at the viewer's back.) The West End Elevated to Coney Island was just completed in 1917. However, this photo feels so contemporary—small businesses are still there, though after much turnover. Today: many more pedestrians, and many fewer parking spaces. Georgette Seminara lived on the other side of the El, almost directly opposite the ICE, COAL and WOOD sign with crossed Italian and American flags. I would bet that iceman Dominick was "barese."

Photo, reproduced with permission, from "Brooklyn's Bensonhurst, Bath Beach, and New Utrecht Communities, a Photographic History," Brian Merlis with Lee A. Rosenzweig. Allen Kent, consultant.

Joseph C. Polacco

A cold trip to Rockefeller Center enroute to an East Side French restaurant for a lunch with cousins Janie Harris-Monti and David Monti. Mom was convinced that we paid a heavy surcharge for the French accents.

18. A Trip to the Cancer Center

Yes, when I didn't have a ride I would take the West End to visit Mom at Maimonides. But today, a chemo day in the first of her two regimes, Mom was home, I was in town to accompany her, and we had a ride. Mom probably feigned a positive attitude, though I knew she was dreading chemo, so she went to the session in "good spirits." We both knew she agreed to chemo to please me. Mom always was an early riser, and especially so for today's session. I was lifted from my bed by the aroma of her espresso; we always said demitasse—why? And, as usual, she had been quiet as a mouse so I could squeeze in a few extra moments of sleep. I straggled out of the spare room to "Joseph, I have your coffee; do you want a bialy?" I saw no discordance in the juxtaposition of Italian espresso and the Jewish bialy.

Sandy La Pazza was our ride, and showed up early to take us to the Maimonides Cancer Center. "C'mon, I wanna get dere before alternate parking is ovah so I can gedda spot!"

Before we could gedda spot near Maimonides, we *had* to make a stop at Mom's bank on 86th Street, right there in the midst of the open-air markets. She had a $28 refund check to cash. A new teller asked for ID, the account number not being sufficient, and instructed Mom to go to the manager for approval. After waiting twenty-five minutes to speak to the woman—mannaggia! An acquaintance even! The check was approved. Upon returning to the teller, he asked, "How do you want it?" and Mom said, "In hundreds!" The new teller was a charming, tall and slim Afro-Latino, and Vina greeted him in future encounters with a "Hiya handsome!" They soon became very tight and, later, whenever I handled Mom's business at the bank, he always asked for her.

Sandy was apoplectic, but we made our way to the Cancer Center.

What can be said of a room in which people are arrayed in a circle, reclining on folding lounge chairs, with semi-poisonous fluids dripping into an arm—folks accompanied by loved ones, folks with unknown expiration dates? The first time I entered this sanctum, I was prepared for a morbid experience. However, it wasn't, really. It was just a reminder of our mortality, and of being kind to each other while we can. Indeed, there was not even a guarantee that those tending to loved ones would actually outlast them. In this reverie about a celebration of mortality, and an opportunity to squeeze out the sweetness of life while we can, my rose-colored glasses were shattered. Naked eyes saw that some patients could not stand up after a session, and some loved ones gave in to sobbing.

Mom was always positive and talkative. She often showed up with crocheted hats for the Cancer Center gift shop. Her own pate was stylishly covered in her creations. On this day we were fortunate to see Dr. Lech Dabrowski, Mom's oncologist. Earlier, upon learning I had a PhD in Biochemistry, he henceforth addressed me as Professor, and provided reports, mainly via fax and phone conversations. We would soon go to a second chemo regime; the taxol of the first regime was being overcome by resourceful cancer cells—the levels of the oncogenic markers, the self-same markers from the original breast lump removed eight years before, were inexorably rising. Vina was cancer-free for close to seven years, but in this belated recurrence we already knew about metastasis to bone.

Dr. D enjoyed Mom. She had all her marbles, and she made him laugh. She was brave in an understated way. So, they chatted. "Mrs. D'Agostino (properly pronouncing DAHGO-stino in his Polish accent), all of your vital signs are good, your blood chemistry is excellent, and I can't believe that a woman of eighty-six years is not on any medication."

"Yes," she said, "I'm in great health, except that I have cancer."

Later, having bid farewell to Dr. D, fellow chemo travelers, the ladies at the front desk, and the cancer support group women on the first floor, we set out on the streets of Borough Park. It's a sunny day and Mom is going to take the bus—the heck with calling Sandy, and who needs the expense of car service? We walk, arm in arm, along 10th Avenue from 48th Street to catch the 60th Street B9 bus, having left a mostly Hasidic neighborhood for one very Chinese. It seems that everyone is on the street, and that the crowd shares some energizing secret—Brownian motion, if I may be chemical. There is always jostling to get on the bus, to find a seat or at least to position near the exit. Mom complains loudly. Mom had just been through a chemo session, but I am no longer Brooklyn enough to say so: *"Hey, easy buddy, that's my mother, and she just had her chemo. Back off!"* My excuse was not wanting to embarrass Mom.

We move along 60th Street, from 10th to 22nd Avenue (Bay Parkway), and transfer to the B6 Bay Parkway bus to our destination on 77th Street. The bus is half-empty, but near our stop a passenger rushes to the door and nearly floors Mom. "I'm sorry," he says, to which Mom replies to the driver and the other passengers, "No he's not." This was said, not in anger—just a commentary on the human condition. The crowd acquiesced, knowingly.

Home, Mom is resting, but feeling bad for me because she does not have the strength to walk the eleven blocks to buy robbies for my dinner. And she doesn't trust me to avoid getting "robbed" by the wily vendors, or to pick up fresh stuff.

Sandy shows up later, with a dish of robbies and salsiccia over penne—gotta love that woman. Mom doesn't think much of this Sicilian style of robbies, but I eat like eating was just invented.

Rest? The phone rings all afternoon; at first it's friends and relatives all wishing Aunt Vina well, but each conversation ends with Mom asking after the callers. In fact, she was knitting items for new babies in the fold.

She does retire early, but not before lamenting, yet again, that I am leaving my wife alone, and that my work at the University is suffering. I convince her, or try, that my job suffers especially when I'm *there*.

Good night Ma, from your youngster, Professor Emeritus Joe.

Is there an exciting conclusion to this story? My recounting tells me how precious these experiences were, and how Mom probably hid so much pain from me to make my schlep from Mid-Missouri to Brooklyn worthwhile.

But, the chemo issue never rested. Dr. D was very into the regimes, and was up on the latest chemo agents. Complicating Mom's condition was that her form of breast cancer was triple-negative, or TNBC, simply meaning that it lacked each of the three receptors for hormones and growth factors found in other types. These receptors can be specifically targeted, while TNBC requires a more general chemical warfare, or waves of combinations of chemo agents. Usually TNBC has a higher relapse rate, I learned in retrospect. So, being cancer-free for almost seven years after her lumpectomy and radiation was unusual, and in some ways a positive—perhaps we'd caught it in time. But the late recurrence in Mom's case was equally worrisome, because the resurgent cancer cells had a chance to metastasize "under the radar." Also, Mom was not as vigilant as she should have been in the latter part of those seven years of remission. Mom was quite frank and typically comical about why she hated mammograms.

Among my duties at the University of Missouri, I teach general biochemistry to pre-med students. I love to explain biochemical aspects of chemotherapy. So, while I could intellectually engage Dr. D on chemo modes of action, and the assays for the tumor markers, the situation was that Mom was suffering the anguish of being very sick, and suffering the effects of the chemo. She was also very Catholic: Suicide is a mortal sin, and so she would not accept any kind of palliative exit out. So, she endured, and a lot of it was for my sake. I realized that, and tried to weigh the desire of seeing Mom well against not wanting to extend her suffering. My Laura, Nonny's "love divine" grand-daughter, was dead-set against the chemo, and she made excellent arguments. She was a Phi Beta Kappa Society member at

Berkeley in Molecular and Cell Biology, and used her smarts and steel trap logic to back me into a corner. Other folks were also dead-set against chemo. None of this was easy, but it was not about me.

When it was clear that the second round was also becoming ineffective, and when metastasis to bone was obvious, we gave up the chemo. Bone-reinforcing medication was in order, and Mom suffered no bone pain beyond the insults imparted on her spinal column over the years of walking, lifting, bending, and falling. These were the best days of the last days, actually. A notable exception was a horrible night in the Maimonides emergency room—dealing with the consequences of the cancer spreading to her stomach.

I was in Brooklyn because Dr. D had called to say Mom's cancer had spread to her stomach. I decided that I should not give her this "stomach news" over the phone, so I flew back that same day, unannounced. I called her from LaGuardia to announce my arrival, and that I would set up my own bed that night. When she realized that I called from the airport and not from Missouri, she yelled "Stay away! Leave me alone!" This was so out of character, and I felt worse than useless, rather like another stab at Mom. Georgette told me that I could stay with her, but in her wisdom she advised that I "let Mom be for a while," and then call back. I followed her advice, arrived at the apartment, and it was sweet.

I waited two days to give her the news, face to face, both of us seated. She looked me in the eye and asked "is it (the stomach cancer) malignant?" I said it was, and that was settled. We had a wonderful time together for the rest of my stay until, of course, the bleeding episode. That long night in the Emergency Room, I got very close to Georgette's Greek neighbors. That long night they eventually learned they lost a loved one.

Superstorm Sandy had inundated and closed many Brooklyn ERs, so the patient overflow crowded Maimonides and it *really* became a zoo. I do not want to re-live some of those very low moments. Mom deserved much better than to be next to a Latin Kings style gang-banger in the overflow area. One could tell he was *malo*, not only from his mouth—one of the few times I wished I did not understand Spanish—but also from his police accompaniment.

Joseph C. Polacco

Of course, on the way from her apartment to the ER, Mom's spirit came through. This woman, who had just vomited a seemingly huge amount of blood into a pail, had the presence of mind to tell me to call an ambulance, and questioned my wanting to flush her stools, 'cause they could be useful for analysis of her condition. The ambulance driver was a latino, his EMT partner an Italian woman, and they worked exceptionally well together; with care they placed her on a gurney for transport. After trying to convince them that she did not need to lie down, Mom told them to make sure she was secure. The driver told her, "You're a feisty one," and indeed, we made conversation all the way to Maimonides. Enough about the ER.

I think hospice was one of the best times of the "end times." To be sure, there was dealing with Medicare, insurance, home versus in-patient hospice, and all the other decision-making that came up. Plus, Mom was fearful of burning up whatever inheritance Michael and I would share. But, at the end, we met some very caring people. Mom and I really got to speak about topics I would not have touched even months before: "Joseph, so many people die anonymously—on the battlefield, in unmarked mass graves—why should you go through the expense of a casket and a burial? Do I really need to be next to grandma? How about cremation?" This was said just before the 2012 season's last episode of her favorite TV show, *Downton Abbey*. This was the last episode she saw.

Vina and Joe at Mom's eighty-seventh Birthday, May 25, 2012. She was still in the first phase of chemo, and lost her hair, which returned in a stylish "buzz" during the second round. We were at Sandy's for the surprise party—which Mom thoroughly enjoyed. This was her last birthday celebration.

19. The Fading Light

I think of "Do not go gentle into that good night," the poem by Dylan Thomas. He follows with

> Old age should burn and rave at close of day;
> Rage, rage against the dying of the light.

This was not Vina, she did tread life with energy, but her exit was soft and tender—she did not want to be too much of burden on friends and loved ones, and I am sure she was consumed with how well her boys would be taken care of. And she hated the idea that I would have to deal with clearing out and selling her apartment. I got on the West End only nineteen years after Mom did. Perhaps, since my stop is not that far down the tracks, and since so many of Mom's fellow travelers have already gotten off, I was spurred to put together these stories. Indeed, "exiting" during the compiling of the stories were Julie de Ramo and Sol Schwartz. And Marie D'Agostino just got off. I treasure their words, and being able to pass them on before they moved on. They are extensions of Vina.

Today, I received the following from Goodreads.com:

> That's what literature is. It's the people who
> went before us, tapping out messages from the past,

from beyond the grave, trying to tell us about life
and death! Listen to them!

—Connie Willis, Hugo and Nebula Award-winning writer of
science fiction

I do not purport to have written literature. My goal, wherever
possible, was to use the testimony of those that Mom illuminated.
Many of those testimonies are incredibly poignant and expressive—
the literature of sincerity. Since many of Vina's fellow travellers
are no longer around, I have tried to portray her light from the
more indirect reflections of others, and from my own memory.
So, I cannot guarantee that the whole spectrum of Mom's light
has been projected—my own memory dims, but just writing and
reminiscing and fact-checking blows smoldering embers to life, and
these memories shed light on other stories. I hope that the smoke
has not obscured the complete picture, and I cannot always vouch
for all the details. While my scientist's obsessive desire for accuracy
gnaws at me, for the purpose of painting the environment of Mom/
Aunt Vina, insignificant details do not matter. Vina would have
been my perfect source for fact-checking—she could recite gnarly
family relationships effortlessly, and showed impatience when I
would ask her to slow down so I could write out a family tree, or
recall incidents.

Unstated were the internalized pain and many dark situations that
Mom endured, situations in which Mom's light really shone through.
However, I do not want to resuscitate those dark memories, nor
besmirch others in the process. Speaking of dark, I used to think
that only Italian families had skeletons and the malocchio, until
I attended an Ivy League school, and learned that WASP families
could be even weirder. Stephen King just reinforces that notion.
So, this is yet another reason, dear reader, not to be depressingly
familiar with darker sides that are in all of our lives. Just as plants
thrive under light/dark cycles, so do marriages—yes, a dangerous
jump from plant physiology to marital relationships, and no charge

for my insights. Mom and Stepdad both emitted light, sometimes completely out of phase, other times in phase, to a reinforced mutual light.

I also wanted to emphasize that our Vina had real strength and endurance—*aguante*, as my Nancy would say in her native Spanish. And through Mom's travails, I am just amazed at how much she shielded my brother and me; how she knew the details of mob hits, infidelities, domestic violence, family tragedies and assaults—some on her character—and just kept it all within, or at least away from my brother and me. Mom's sources were relatives, 86th Street vendors and, of course, the chiacchierone and *yentas* (gossipers) at the sewing machines of the neighborhood dress shops. Michael and I lived in her light, not her shadow.

The neighborhood itself was like our extended family, and there was much common knowledge. But in the old days, the neighborhood had its own omertà with outsiders. It probably still does. On a visit home from grad school, I witnessed a police forensic unit taking samples from a murder, an assault that occurred on my Bay 31st and 86th Street corner, just a half-block from a neighborhood bar. The victim was a young Chinese guy, and in those days, the only Chinese in the 'hood ran restaurants or hand laundries. So, both the crime and the victim were unusual; neighborhoods where the mob had a presence were usually "quiet." I told my stepdad that he needed to talk to the police, and he assured me that "We'll take care of this." I don't know how much he knew, and I never knew the upshot. While I wanted to see justice meted out, I am not sure if the punishment would have been the same had a paisan been "whacked" in an unsanctioned "hit."

Harking back to even older days, there were indeed Chinese residents of Bensonhurst. When Stepdad bought our two-story building, the first tenants living over our store were a Chinese couple and their two girls. They were Catholic, and I easily recall the young ladies in their white first communion dresses. Willie, the dad, played jazz sax in Chinatown in his youth. The mom was a housewife, I believe, and was my mom's good buddy. Being a chiacchierona knew no ethnic bounds. They owned a neighborhood Chinese restaurant; we ate there on summer Wednesday evenings. I recall Stepdad jokingly commiserating with Willie over the "five-star general," his mother-in-law, in the kitchen. Every Christmas, even after Willie and family moved out, we got a box of delicacies, including lychee nuts and candied kumquats. I encouraged Stepdad to reciprocate with a provolone or prosciutto, but he considered the gift a one-way tribute to the old landlord.

In addition to restaurants, there were the "Chinese Hand Laundries"—one right around our corner, next to Tony's Barber Shop, yes, on Bay 31st Street. They were not self-service; they offered full-service laundering only. The establishments were Spartan, artless, utterly functional—floor-to-ceiling shelves of finished laundry, folded and wrapped in brown paper. Steam and noise emanated from behind a curtain leading to the back. You left off your shirts, maybe pants, with instructions on how much starch, de-staining, etcetera. Don't lose that ticket—this was the origin of "no tick-ee, no shirt-ee." The old guy who met the public knew where every package was. He looked like an emaciated Ho Chi Minh in a tank top (old man's sleeveless ribbed T-shirt—official Chinese Bocce uniform), sporting a wispy, unkempt goatee and always greeting me with a "Hello, bigga boy."

Stepdad fancied himself a "man of respect," and indeed he was—a successful 86th Street merchant and a Kiwanian—but he was not "mobbed up." However, he did not rein in people's imaginations, and his getting more sartorial as he aged probably further stoked those imaginations. At times, a few people asked him for "favors." I know he interceded on behalf of debtors, folks who were having trouble with the *vig*, or "juice," usurious interest on loans from sharks. In the old days, sharks were more commonly "Shylocks." Indeed, some of the creditors were Jewish, but the ones I knew of were all paisans. And Stepdad's good deeds got him face-to-face with some very dangerous creditors. Again, I will not mention names, but this was a "dark side" to Mom. She was very much afraid that her husband would, well, over-step, and then there would be hell to pay, plus

Joseph C. Polacco

the vig. Mom sure could scold "Louie D," using no uncertain street vernacular.

Before I leave the subject of playing on the edge, and being sartorial: Stepdad, accompanied by Mom, attended a "showing" at the Cusimano and Russo Funeral Home on West 6th Street, just across the street from Nonna Nunziatina's Avenue T apartment. The Home is an ornate structure; it recalls the architecture of the Corleone mansion on Long Island. Capo Carlo Gambino was among the mourners on this occasion, though I am not sure that he and Stepdad were paying their respects to the same deceased person—C & R has several individual visitation parlors. In any case, upon leaving Stepdad grabs his overcoat, and is nervously told that it belongs to il Capo. So, he takes it off and puts it back on the hanger, grabs his own, and says something like, "I was wondering who the cheapskate was; there were only two quarters in the pockets." Don Carlo was an avuncular type, at least in appearance, and Stepdad could turn on the humor and charm, so any confrontation, to my thinking, would have been quickly defused.

Respect was important in the culture of Bensonhurst, and la famiglia. After my postdoctoral in 1974, starting my first real job, our young family of five moved into our own house in Hamden, Connecticut. Mom actually made it out there to visit, the first time with Toni Caggiano and Large Mary, and she sobbed before getting out of the car. Stepdad lent me the down-payment, and we scrimped for over a year to make the first installment on the loan—no vig here. I asked my older boy, four-year-old Joseph, to present his grandfather with an envelope containing $1,000 cash—Italian style. Stepdad opened the envelope, examined the contents, and later returned the cash, telling me in private that the most important thing to him was "respect."

Late in her life, as Mom's own light was flickering, she and I talked much more seriously than we ever had, and about darker subjects. During her Great Depression-era childhood, she witnessed a boarder making a move on her mother—my Nonna took on two boarders to make ends meet. One was a perfect gentleman, and the other not. The first "arranged" for the second to leave. Stories such as these just ebbed from Mom over the years, and more so in her last year. I never set out to unearth such oral histories. They rose to the surface on occasion. For example, one of our 86th Street neighbors was an attractive Sicilian immigrant woman. Though the woman was a grandmother, I could sense her earthiness in my awakening adolescence. According to Mom *A signora* killed her boyfriend in the old country because her Mafioso husband gave her two choices: "You kill him, or I kill you."

Mom also increasingly let on that she had to leave my biological father, the love of her life, because of his compulsive gambling, and the things that gambling debts, loan sharks, and the vig could lead a debtor to do. Gambling may seem one of the lesser sins, but it is the impetus for many larger ones. Mom painted a potential murder-suicide scene from page two of the *National Enquirer*—a consequence of her staying too long with my biological father. Trying to pay off his gambling debts got him into a federal prison where, by the way, he edited the prison newspaper and wrote poetry to Vina. So, for her boys' sake, Mom left Mike Polacco and eventually embraced Lou D'Agostino.

Stepdad was suffering emotionally from being estranged from his wife. He managed a ladies' handbag factory in which Vina was one of the operators. Two relationships rent asunder leave four festering, frayed ends. But Mom was able to weave together a Lou-Vina relationship that lasted fifty years. She endured much recrimination during the process. This was darkness that she kept from Michael and me. She felt that Lou would be good for her boys, and she was right about that. And, Mom was good for Lou's biological kids as well, though they resisted her mightily at first. Stepdad's biological kids never lived with us on a permanent basis, but we had frequent interactions.

So, Vina embraced Lou and the D'Agostino clan, and in so doing cut herself off from the Polaccos. The families were akin to parallel universes, with no mutual knowledge of each other, much less communication, though we shared the same "space." However, I recall one incident when Mom relented, and contact was made. I

Joseph C. Polacco

was about eight years-old and was taken to see Aunt Nancy who lived within a block of Nonna Nunziatina on the same side of Avenue T. At first, I could not understand why this woman and her daughter were so emotional, and showed me so much affection, but later I had no problem abiding Mom's strident admonition: "Don't tell Daddy [Lou]!" Nancy is Mike Polacco's sister. Other than this incident, Mom and Mike's kids had no contact with the Polaccos. She did not want to arouse Lou's jealousies, nor see Mike in dire straits. She cut the emotional and financial ties and child support was a foreign concept, one I never heard exit Mom's lips.

Mike was not at Aunt Nancy's that day, and I learned only very recently that he became a pariah for much of the family. I made telephone contact with cousin Joanne, Nancy's daughter. She was there that day on Avenue T. We are now in our mid to late 70's and I hope we soon reconnect in the flesh. Our passing ships have passed signals to each other.

I have two, possibly constructed, memories of Mike Polacco—the first in the Spumoni Gardens, already mentioned, at the 25th Ave stop of the West End. The second was in Nonna's Avenue T apartment. I believe Mom and I were there before our living arrangement "stabilized" after Mom's escape. He showed up and I was happily in Poppa Mike's arms again. Mike was his jovial self while Mom had tears in her eyes—the contrasting emotions must have burned into my memory, though no doubt Mike was also dying inside.

Aunt Nancy and Poppa Mike are now long-gone. On one of my Brooklyn visits in Mom's last year, I came across my first cousin Joe, yes, another Joe Polacco. We first made contact on Facebook, how prosaic. I sought him out at his place of work. Cuz Joe is the son of the late Tony Polacco, the third of the three siblings. Joe's wife Sandra connected me with cousin Joanne—for which I am most grateful.

Each of the three orphaned Polacco siblings had two kids. One each of Tony's and Nancy's survives and Vina's two boys, sons of kid bro Mike, are still kicking. I am trying to kick up as much trouble as I can before I call it a day. I know Vina approves. But, forgive me, Ma, for also kicking up unhappy memories.

I do not mean to make negative comparison of the Polaccos vis-à-vis the D'Agostinos. Going back another generation, to my paternal grandparents, reveals a gripping example of strong family ties. Joseph and Rose Polacco emigrated from Gravina in Puglia, near Bari, and died in America, almost a hundred years ago, victims of the influenza pandemic, leaving three young orphans. According to Mom, siblings and in-laws on both sides of the marriage, and the Atlantic, came together in various arrangements, including a staged wedding, to adopt the kids—Nancy (b.1911), Tony (b. 1916 or 1917), and baby Michael Polacco. The epidemic struck in 1918–1920, and Mike was born in 1918, so he made it "under the wire."

And, according to Mom, the Polaccos were part of the *Baresi* fun-loving and spirited immigrant community, concentrated in New Jersey (Metuchen?). While Mike Polacco may have been more a man of letters (and probably numbers and daily double odds), the *Baresi* in general made their way into more labor-intensive occupations. There was an early entry into the coal business, when coal furnaces heated buildings and homes. Then, they were big in the ice business, when folks had ice-boxes, before the electric Frigidaires of Bess Myerson. Finally, or at least next, they became movers in the paper industry—I am not talking journalism, but papers for printing and photocopying. Go figure the logical thread. And, I wonder if they had to use "muscle" to garner market share (duhhhh).

And Bari itself worked its way into my professional life. I have wonderful colleagues at the *Università degli Studi di Bari*, Ferdinando and Luigi Palmieri. They are superb scientists, and have always treated Nancy and me as family. Being Barese on my father's side did not hurt. Bari was *beautiful*—it reminded me of old-time Brooklyn, with families in the streets 'til the wee hours, feasting on pizza, gelato, sfogliatelle; sipping coffee and wine. The Adriatic in the moonlight could have been Gravesend Bay. *Vide'o mare quant'è bello, spira tantu sentimentoooooooo...* Okay, okay, that

Joseph C. Polacco

was for Sorrento, Bay of Naples, but I *am* Barese-Napoletano.

Once, while passing time in Ferdinando's office, I picked up a phone book and found a Polacco in Bisceglia—a paese next door, the hometown of Marie D'Agostino's father. Mom was thrilled that I visited the old sod, and on several occasions. I wanted to take her to Italy, put it off too long, and then her suddenly declining health intervened. If she loved Spain, which she adored, she would have felt like she had gone to heaven in Italy.

In fact, there is virtual unanimity that Mom is there now, and is looking down on us. As indicated in chapter 7, Georgette is convinced that Mom pulled some strings so that a memorial mass and a reception in her memory—organized by Toni Caggiano and Denise Daniello—would come off smoothly at the Holy Family Home. By now you know, dear reader, that Toni is one of Vina's many "nieces." Denise, an assistant manager at the home, interacted with Vina almost daily. Denise became "da niece," as well. The reception and the accompanying mass were well-attended, albeit more than three months after Vina's passing—a testimonial to the love and concern she shared with so many. Part of the program follows:

May 31, 2013

Memorial Mass

Feast of the Visitation of the Blessed Virgin Mary

and Reception

For

Vina D'Agostino

Holy Family Home (1740 84th Street, Brooklyn, NY)

You're Still With Me, Ma

Your hand on my back, your strength in my gait
Faced down doubts and fears along my highway
A road your sacrifice and love helped me navigate
You bore pain in your life, so my own found its way

A pain borne, with cheerful love, for all and for me
Though a few of the all exacted a cruel, selfish toll
I could play ball, travel, relish the good life with glee
Only later to realize how most protective your role

And I thank you, Momma, for making me aware
As you were journeying through that final door
That your life was still a long, loving prayer
For my peace and well-being on this earthly shore

Now, you've left me, but left me much stronger
To say I feel alone is but pure heresy
Though your touch I may have no longer
Your loving light guides my own odyssey

As I call a daily "hello," talk as each day unfolds
I feel your love, your unspoken concern
For your Joseph, now become a young 'un old
But I keep your daily passion: to live and to learn

So, Momma, you're my angel and always ensconced
In my firmament, as my compass, my guiding star
Your unselfish love will ever be steady response
To my yearnings and doubts both within and afar

—Joe, May 31, 2013, Holy Family Home

Joseph C. Polacco

But, I can't leave with something so "tear-jerky," or, as Mom would say, "Ancora, still with the water works!" Mom was spicy, vivacious; she would have wanted folks to dance at her reception. On one occasion, Mom arranged for Nancy and me to demo Latino dancing, and actually got some of the Holy Family residents up and wiggling. So, I presented two more verses on this memorial occasion. Momma passed twelve days after St. Valentine's Day, and my Nancy, with her own love, made that sad time bearable:

Valentine's Day, 2013

Baby, vos sos el rosal del jardín de mi alma
Aunque yo enfrente un invierno frio y duro
Tu aroma, calor, y color—antorcha que me calma
Y me muestra escape de este camino oscuro
    —Joe (Te amo hoy y pa' siempre, loquita)

Baby, you're the rose garden of my soul
Though I endure a winter long and stark
Your aroma, heat, and light—a torch I extol
That shows me my road, no longer dark
    —Joe (I love you today and
    forever, crazy li'l ole thing)

And, a few months after Valentine's Day 2013, Brooklyn witnessed the emergence of Brood II of the seventeen-year periodical cicada. (Did I say I like bugs?) To me, these emergences are an example of the mysterious "life force" that has death as an integral part. And, two years before, Missouri witnessed the emergence of our own Brood IX and it inspired me to poetry. Pardon the salty nature of the following limerick. All limericks are salty, or should be. Mom was reverent, but also had a great sense of humor, and always appreciated the salty side of a good joke. So, I was inspired as I saw a young University of Missouri student being "accosted" by a vagabond cicada from our own Missouri brood. The young lady's response was both hysterical and hysterically funny. Mom would have loved it.

Cicader (Midwest for Cicada): Live, Love, Die, Be Reborn

> There once was a randy brand-new cicader
> Sincere, yet a young lady's noisy invader;
>   "Sure, maybe I caused her a rustle
>   buzzed a few times at her bustle
> But, St. Peter, my love was sure to sedate her."

Vina's Designs
CUSTOM FASHIONS & ALTERATIONS

BY APPOINTMENT
(212) 266-8492

I don't think this was the "Designs by Vina" card. The 212 area code could have been pre-1985 Brooklyn. The rest of the number tells me it was for our old home phone. Note the stylized owl.

Glossary

Abuelita: (Spanish) Diminutive for abuela, or grandmother

(Gli) Azzurri: Literally, The Blues, but not the musical kind. Italy, with a *tri-colore* flag of red, white and green, has a national football (soccer) selection clad in blue. Go figure.

Baccalà: Cod fish. When salted and dried, it is sometimes "*Stoccafisso*" or *Stocca Baccalà* (Stock Fish or Stock Cod). How did a cold water fish become so popular in Southern Italy? In the text, I credit the Portuguese for fishing and selling it, but probably initial credit goes to the Vikings/Norwegians who "migrated" to Northern France around 1,000 AD, transmogrified to the Normans, and later finished their conquest of southern Italy (by 1154), bringing the cod habit with them.
Thanks to Wikipedia for this piece of Norman history

Broccoli di rapa: Bitter greens (*Brassica oleraceae*, though this is disputed) of the Brassicaceae (Cruciferae) family that includes broccoli, kale, collards, mustard greens, etcetera. On the street these are affectionately called "robbies" or "broccoli raab."
I recently ordered a side dish of *friarielli* in a family restaurant in Naples, and it was robbies, which the waiter confirmed.

Bruschetta: A simple affair, toasted Italian bread, anointed with olive oil and garlic and garnished with tomatoes, and sometimes other ingredients, such as olives (the good kind). WARNING: Do NOT ask for bru´shetta; the pronunciation is bru´sketta.

Casiolo: Mom's baked zucchine (singular = *zucchina*) with eggs, ricotta, grating cheese, onions and a few other wonderful ingredients.

Calamari: Squid (plural).

Caponatina: Cold eggplant dish, a diminutive of *Caponata*. I believe the name derives from the presence capers (*capperi*) which, in Sicily, are Bunyanesque.

Carogna: Carrion. Probably much more polite than *sfacim*, which refers to a rotten person.

Che peccato: What a pity. *Peccato* is related to the English word, peccadillo (little sin, or indiscretion). *Peccato* can mean both a pity and a sin. *Io ho peccato*: I have sinned.

Che si dice: As a question, literally, "What is being said?" But, in usage in the 'hood, the meaning is more like "What do you say?" or, "Whaddya say?"

Chiacchierare: To gossip. A gossip (n) is a *chiachierone* (or, feminine, *chiachierona*). Some gossips are very critical, and the term Nonna and Mom used for them sounded like *biddicusa* (English phonetics) which I theorize is based on *pidocchiuso*, or lice-ridden. So, think of "nit-picking," or small-minded.

Chooch: Street pronunciation of *ciuccio*—a jackass or stupid person, a patsy. It is also, supposedly, a pacifier—"binky"—but I never heard it used this way in Brooklyn.

Chutzpah: (Yiddish, Hebrew) Temerity, audacity, nerve, cheek.

Compare/Comare: Godfather/Godmother. However, there are shades of meanings, some ironic. *Comare* can be a (wink) girlfriend, and *compare* a comrade, best man, or countryman. The latter is also expressed as *cumpà* (in Naples and elsewhere [Wikipedia]), and probably gave rise to the Anglicized "Goombah," or countryman. To me, *cumpà* is related to *compai* that some Spanish speakers use for comrade or buddy. "The Godfather" of Hollywood is closer to *Il Padrino*.

Cornetto: Literally, "Little Horn," used to help ward off the evil eye/*malocchio/maloik*. It is perhaps best known as a brand name for a frozen ice cream cone, produced in Naples.

Couve: (Portuguese) Yet another blessed member of the "cabbage" (Brassicaceae) family. A leafy green that to me resembles collards.

Cozze: Mussels

Cuchifritos: OH, so bad, and oh, SO good. These are Puerto Rican versions of Spanish deep-fried pork: blood sausage (*morcilla*), meat-stuffed tropical potato "croquettes" (*papas rellenas*), fried pork skin (*chicharrón*). Stop!! I can't go on. A tropical fruit drink with your chicharrón?

Dreidel: (Hebrew) A spinning clay toy, especially popular at Chanukah. Its four sides form a four-letter Hebrew acronym meaning "A Great Miracle Happened Here."

Estofado: (Spanish) Stew, not stuffed, but probably related—easy for me to get stuffed on this, especially in winter months. The Spanish-speaking world has many beautiful stews, *ajiaco* and *sancocho* (Colombia), *puchero* (Uruguay and South America). The list is an alphabet soup of varieties, origins and components. See **Olla podrida.**

Farfariello: Diminutive of *farfalla*, or butterfly. Note that Farfariello masculinized the name. Note also that "bowtie" macaroni in Italian are *farfalle*, because bowties can also appear to be butterflies. (No health code against these insects in your pasta dish.)

Famiglia: Family and, just as for its English cognate, it can mean a nuclear, extended or a "business" family.

Fazool: A term not only to describe beans and macaroni, but also "old-timer" Italians, the ones with the accents. I am not sure of its origin, but I believe it to be an "Italianization" of *fossil*. See **Pasta Fazool**

Feijoada: (Brazilian Portuguese) Literally, "Big Bean Dish," its components are black beans and all of the pig that the slaves could rescue from their masters' kitchens. We would call some of the contents chitterlings, jowls, and feet. This dish has achieved royalty status in Brazil, where most folks eat a little higher on the hog than did the *escravos* (slaves) of old.

Femmina: Woman. *Mala Femmina*, famous song title, is Evil or Bad Woman. *Mala* here is an adjective, and is often joined with nouns, such as *malasorte* (bad luck), or the common *malocchio* (evil/bad eye).

Focaccia: Kinda like pizza, except dough has more leavening. Usually, endowed with olive oil, and savory herbs, such as rosemary. The *sfinciunnu* focaccia is heavenly.

Gavoon: Street form for *cafone*, or peasant. Refers to a "greenhorn" who just got off the boat, unrefined.

Guaglione: A kid, in Neapolitan dialect, and probably elsewhere. *Picciritto* is also used, but I believe for younger kids. A word about Southern Italian dialect: It is NOT homogeneous, and in parts of Sicily *Picciritto* is more like *Picciriddu*.

Giorno del Mio Onomastico: My name saint's day—literally, "Day of my namesake saint." Note how frequent *giorno* is in Italian usage— *buongiorno* (good morning, good day), *buona giornata* (good day), *al giorno d'oggi* (nowadays), *mezzogiorno* (mid-day), etcetera.

Goy: (Yiddish, Hebrew) Non-Jewish, or Gentile

Innamorato: Literally, "in love." Refers to boyfriend (*innamorato*) or girlfriend (*innamorata*). Many *innamorati* visited with us in our in-store Sunday feasts. The price of being an *innamorato* was dinner with the parents and relatives of the parents. *Fidanzato* is more serious, a fiancé.

Judería: (Spanish) "Jewry"—Jews collectively or a Jewish quarter in a town or city.

Kasha: (My guess is a "Yiddish-ized" version of Russian or Polish) Ground, de-hulled buckwheat, hence, a whole grain containing bran and the "germ." Takes some getting used to, and Mom went through a kick where she foisted it on us. Supposedly, Ashkenazy Jews used it as a knish stuffing, and as a part of a "sauce" on farfalle/bow-tie pasta. Ahh, the twains meet (!)

Knaidl: (Yiddish) A dumpling, with variable filling, including kasha and served in a soup. Probably related to the German Knödel dumpling.

Latticini Freschi: (Fresh) milk products. So, in a strict sense, cheese emporia with this name should not offer aged or cured cheeses, but they do. Mozzarella, butter and ricotta are indeed made daily, or frequently, and hence are *bona fide* items for sale. However, if a Latticini Freschi (lah-tee-CHEE-nee FRESS-kee) does not have torpedoes of provolone hanging from the ceiling, and wheels of Parmigiano-Reggiano prominently displayed, and if does not "reek" of cheese, I take my business elsewhere.

Most Latticini Freschi double as a Salumeria. See **Salumeria**.

Magari: Maybe. Sometimes with the intonation of hope.

Mal de ojo: (Spanish) Evil eye. In Portuguese, it's *mal-olhado,* "evil-eyed" or *olho gordo,* "fat eye."

Malocchio: Evil eye (Mal + *occhio* [eye]).

Maloik: *Malocchio* as it's called on the street.

Mannaggia: An expletive, as "dammit," or an adjective, as *Mannaggia'merica* (Damn America). The latter expression was used so much by the old-timers, that I thought "America" in Italian was *Mannaggia'merica*. Note that very few were moved enough to return to *Mannaggia'talia*.

Maronna: Literally, Large Mary or Mother, or Madonna. *Maronna Mia* is a common expression, so much so, that it is hardly considered "using the Lord's name in vain."

Mensch: (Yiddish) Obviously a man, one who has come of age. Note that "man" in English is related to "human," and so a mensch has grown up to be an adult human, in the best sense of the word.

Mezzogiorno: Literally, mid-day, or noon, it refers to Southern Italy, the Italy south of Rome. To me south of Rome is probably morning, not the benighted region some may associate with Naples, Bari, Sicily, etcetera. The Mezzogiorno is sometimes termed *Zona Meridionale* meaning, at least to me, the "morning" of Italy. Much of the Mezzogiorno was part of *Graecia Magna*, or "Greater Greece" at its apex.

Archimedes was born and died Siracusa, Sicily (287 – ca. 210 BC), though he spent a significant amount of time in enlightened Alexandria, Egypt.

Minestrone: Italian vegetable soup, whose contents vary with available vegetables. *Minestra* is soup, and *minestrone* is a "big," or hearty, soup.

Mortifam: Anglicization of *Morte di fame* (dying of starvation). Bensonhurst usage indicated someone, like an adolescent, looking to eat anything in sight. At times, freeloader, or mooch. See **Schnorrer**.

Mozzarella: Cheese produced by rennin action on components of the milk protein, casein. Rennin is a digestive, curdling protein from the fourth stomach of the cow, or any cud-chewing animal. Upon rennin action, proteins coagulate and precipitate.

Water buffalo milk makes the best mozzarella, and there is a thriving industry in Naples, Sicily and parts of South America. The whey, or remaining liquid, is the source of *ricotta*.

Mui gavarim pa-ruuski: (transliterated Russian) "We speak Russian (here)." This is the Russian version of "Aqui se habla español" or "Qui si parla italiano."

(La) Moda: Fashion

Nella cucina: Simply, "in the kitchen," but when the kitchen is such a central place of tradition and reverence, the Italian operatic version seems more appropriate.

Ochin xharascho: (transliterated Russian) "Very good" or "very well."

Olla podrida: (Spanish) Literally, "rotten pot," with the meaning of a stew of many possible ingredients. This term is also used figuratively, as in the first chapter.

Omertà: "No snitching." Code of silence among illegal (or secret) societies.

Oy gefilte: (Yiddish) The second word means, to me at least, "stuffed fish" (gefilte fish) such as whiting—a junk fish the Jews tried to gussy up. *Oy gefilte* is a mild blasphemy, and intimates exasperation. My take is that gefilte is a pedestrian food, and so *oy gefilte* can also be a response to one making something of out a triviality.

Pasta fazool: Anglicization of "*Pasta con fagioli*," (macaroni and beans). See **Fazool.**

Pazzo: Crazy. Pronounced POTS-oh. The English say "potty" (the adjective) and I think it's related. Yes, I am *pazzo* over etymology.

Polpo: Octopus. In dialect, or on the streets, "ee BOOP." (When I hear of Betty Boop, I always think of octopus.)

Pueblo de los Estados Unidos: (Spanish) People of the U.S.A.

Ragazza: Girl. This is more standard Italian. *Raggazzo* is a boy, and a young guy in Naples could be called *guaglione,* a young boy, *picirrillo,* or *picciriddo. Picciriddu* is Sicilian. Now, a young girl? I am hesitant to suggest *piccirrilla,* since it might have negative connotations.

Ricotta: Literally, "re-cooked." A cheese made from the whey in the production of mozzarella. Proteins remaining in the whey are brought down by acidification (vinegar), and heat. Cottage cheese is made directly from milk, leaving the whey. I do not think there is an etymological relationship between ricotta and cottage cheese.

Ruffiano: A "two-faced" person, one who uses charm to ingratiate, but whose intentions are not pure. A good synonym, at least for some uses, is *vigliacco*—a cowardly and/or contemptible person, a rogue or scoundrel. The latter was a favorite of Jim Mangano's dad, while Vina preferred the (probably) milder, *ruffiano*. See **Schifoso** and **Sfacim**.

Salsiccia: Fresh pork sausage, hot and "sweet." These are the Italian equivalent of Spanish chorizos, and are wonderful in a crusty sandwich, accompanied by cooked bell peppers and onions. See **Salumeria**.

Salumeria: A store (sometimes, simply, "Pork Store") that offers pork products, both preserved and fresh. Fresh sausage (*salsiccia*), when made from pork butt, is excellent, and lean. A thinner (in cross-section) fresh variety, mixed with cheese, is offered in a 2-D spiral, skewered on sticks.

Salted, cured and aged products—cold cuts—are myriad: *capicola (capocollo* and variants*), mortadella, prosciutto* (cured and cooked), *salami* (Genoa and others), *soppressata*, etcetera. In Italy, *pepperone* is a large, or bell, pepper, and NOT a salami. Cold cuts differ in preparation and cut. For example, capocollo is "head" (*capo*) plus "neck" (*collo*) meat. Even tissue source of fat can vary—the hard fat in mortadella is from the neck.

Salumi are preserved, salted pork (and sometimes beef) delicatessen items, and they are offered in a salumeria.

Scassicazzo/Scassigazzo: A real pain; refers to a person. "*Cazzo*" in southern dialects sounds like "Gazzo," and, literally, means penis. So, the reader may infer the kind of pain a so-named person is.

Schlep: (Yiddish, German) To carry something, or one's self, arduously, as in, "Oy I schlepped these books all the way to school, and I didn't need them today."

Schifoso: Loathsome, from *schifare* to loathe. On the street a *schviazzo* is <u>really</u> loathsome, and it sounds like "ski-VOTZ."

Schnorrer: (Yiddish, German) Beggar, sponge or freeloader—one always on the receiving end.

Schnozz: Nose, a loving diminutive of *Schnozzola,* which was a Jimmy Durante trademark. Jimmy was a one-man duet: he and his nose. *Naso,* in Tuscan, is too tame, but the noses *are* larger in the Mezzogiorno.

I have a theory: When Jimmy signed off "Good night Mrs. Kalabash" he was referring to an old love (wife), one he affectionately called "Googootz," which is a calabash, in English.

Semolina: Flour of durum, or hard (*grano duro*) wheat. Semolina flour is preferred for pasta, definitely not for pastry. Semolina bread is readily available in Bensonhurst bakeries, *panetterie.* Durum wheat is an ancient tetraploid, while most modern wheat is hexaploid (*Triticum aestivum*), though there are many grades of *T. aestivum,* which vary in protein content and quality.

But, if it's gluten you're after, go no further than semolina.

Scungilli: Neapolitan dialect for conch, or *sconsiglio.*

Seppia: Cuttlefish. Also a source of ink to make black pasta (*pasta nera*). Likely etymologically related to "sepia" in old, and old-fashioned, black and white photos and film.

Sfacim: A shortened version of *disfacimento,* decayed, but often used in the sense of semen, or rotting carcass, or "scum of the earth." This was not used in *Vina,* and was rarely used by Vina. References to folks who might qualify for the epithet have been expunged. Nonna Nunziatina's English vocabulary was limited, and so she resorted to *sfacim* on frequent occasions.

Sfingi: Ricotta-filled (cannoli cream) deep-fried dough, which is made with pastry flour, milk, eggs and vanilla. Sfingi are usually topped with orange slices and dried, and not nearly as decadent as they appear. I am not sure of the singular—*sfingio?*—and just as well, cause I can't eat just one. **Zeppole and Sfingi** and are both traditional St. Joseph Day (March 19) pastries, but available all year round in Bensonhurst and most of Brooklyn. I recommend both Alba's Pastry Shop on 18th Avenue and 70th Street and Mondial Bakery on 20th Avenue and 78th Street.

Sfinciunnu: This is usually a term for Sicilian Pizza—the thicker bread, with an onion and breadcrumb topping (that can also contain anchovies, and possibly tomatoes). To me, and what do I know, I'm a napoletano-barese, it describes the onion/bread crumb topping to pizza or to focaccia.

Stocca Baccalà (Stoccafisso): See **Baccalà**

Stracciatella: Literally, small rags, which is the appearance of the egg and leafy vegetable component of this delicious soup. Nonna and Vina blessed it with tiny meatballs. The greens could be *chicoria*, dandelion greens from the backyard. A college friend looked down at this dish, a swirling impressionist lacy mélange of yellows (egg), green (chicoria), and tan (cheese), and told me, in his Virginia accent: "Joe, do you know what this looks like?" He has regretted that comment ever since, and even more so for not even trying the dish.

Vina Forgives him.

Oh yes, Stracciatella is also a gelato flavor, but a gelato even the most conservative Virginians will try.

Strega: Witch. Also a yellow-colored liquor, produced in Benevento, which I believe is my maternal great-grandfather's hometown, near Naples (Campania).

Stunad: Stupid person; stupor, as in brain fog.

Vecchiaia: Old age. Some citations are given as "A Vecchiaia," which is dialect (La Vecchiaia in modern Italian). And, properly "A vecchiaia è na carogna" should be "La vecchiaia è una carogna."

Vergogna: Shame, as in "what a shame," which overlaps one of the meanings of *peccato*.

Verrazzano Bridge: A lovely suspension bridge (completed, 1964) that spans the "Narrows" between Staten Island and Brooklyn, the stretch earlier plied by the "Brooklyn-Staten Island Ferry." Giovanni da Verrazzano sailed under the French flag. He was overshadowed by Magellan and others, including Englishman Henry Hudson who sailed the eponymous Hudson River. Rhode Island's Jamestown-Verrazzano Bridge and Maryland's Verrazzano Bridge also honor Don Giovanni, both spanning waters that he sailed.

And, history tends to recycle: according to Wikipedia Verrazzanno is credited with discovering Cape Cod Bay, but the bay's name was *not* changed to *Capo Baccalà*.

I include this entry to:

1. CORRECT the spelling of Verrazzano's name (double "Z");
2. Point out that Verrazzano was the first post-Norse European to 'discover' New York Harbor (500 years later, in 1524); and
3. Remind readers that the "V" bridge traffic flow was within Vina's power, according to Georgette.

Vongole: Clams. The text indicates "cherrystone," which they are, in Brooklyn. In Naples and Sicily a different species populates your pasta.

(La) Vucciria: "Madhouse" in Sicilian dialect(s). Also, the title of a 1974 painting by Renato Guttuso, in which he depicts the old Palermo marketplace, informally called "The Madhouse."

Yenta: (Yiddish) Gossip, busybody. See **Chiacchierare**.

Zeppole (accent on the first syllable): Similar to sfingi, but custard-filled, and topped with a bitter cherry. Northern Italians tend to favor the custard filling; some day civilization will spread further north. (Singular, Zeppola?) Zeppole and Sfingi are both traditional St. Joseph Day (March 19) pastries, but available all year round in Bensonhurst and most of Brooklyn. I recommend both Alba's Pastry Shop on 18th Avenue and 70th Street, and Mondial Bakery on 20th Avenue and 78th Street.

Joe's Bari collaborators that Mom never got to meet. Luigi Palmieri, in Polignano a Mare, hometown of Domenico Modugno of "Volare" fame.

Photos courtesy Polacco family

Roberto Arrigoni and Ferdinando Palmieri flanking Joe; note the Barese family resemblances.

Joseph C. Polacco

A rare candid shot of Stepdad in the late 1950s well before his sartorial phase. He and Mom are both reacting to a Polaroid. His body language, smile, horned-rim glasses and semi-bald pate are all endearing.

Photos courtesy Polacco family

Yes, I have children outside of my marriage. Paco was a surprise birthday present to me, and we mutually imprinted and bonded. He lives now with Mary Schaeffer.

Son Joseph's 2009 wedding in Tomales California. Mom, Joe, Nancy. Linda Kim was and is the lucky bride.

Nancy and I have just celebrated our eleventh anniversary. This photo was taken at the Columbia home of Domingo Martinez and Corinne Valdivia, about a year before our nuptials.

Joseph C. Polacco

Photos courtesy Polacco family

Each time I see a scene like this, I am reminded of Jim Mangano's psalm: "It's great to be Italian." Nancy, Rosalie, Jim and I were enjoying a "light" lunch at Joe's Focacceria on Avenue U and McDonald Ave, not far from Mom's birthplace on Lake Street in the Gravesend Neighborhood.

Sunday dinner with Nonna. When we ate at our place, Nonna brought enough food to feed a traveling circus. Here, I was thinking I should be outside playing stickball instead of gorging, but the food was *so* good, and Nonna so charming. She claimed that as a very young child I spoke Italian with her, and would get angry when I was not completely following her stories as a fifteen year-old.

Easy to see that Joseph was always the more serious of the Polacco brothers. We were tykes of about eight and five.

Photos courtesy Polacco family

Joseph C. Polacco

Acknowledgments

Tremendous thanks are due Vina's friends and fellows without whom there would be no *Vina*. You are generous contributors and collaborators. I am indebted also, for your excavating relevant family photos from your archives. And, speaking of collaborators, thanks to my colleagues at the University of Missouri for covering me while I was making my Brooklyn pilgrimages. My wife Nancy Malugani put up with my being tethered even more than usual in front of a computer screen. She offered very practical advice, well beyond first prodding me to recognize Vina's inner light.

Thanks to Yolanda Ciolli, of AKA-Publishing, who oversaw my transition from a writer of scientific articles to someone resembling an author of memoirs. She taught to me to eschew heavy footnotes and (over-)use of parentheses. The reader wants to read—what great advice!

Melody Kroll is my literary angel. She kept insisting I could write, in spite of my doubts and examples to the contrary. I am still not completely convinced she is right, but if you don't give up, Mel, neither will I.

https://josephpolacco.me
https://ipg.missouri.edu/faculty/polacco.cfm

CPSIA information can be obtained
at www.ICGtesting.com
Printed in the USA
FFHW02n0116200918
48368354-52206FF

9 781942 168577